THE HIDDEN INJURIES OF CLASS

THE
HIDDEN
INJURIES
OF CLASS

by RICHARD SENNETT
and JONATHAN COBB

VINTAGE BOOKS
A Division of Random House
New York

Library of Congress Cataloging in Publication Data
Sennett, Richard, 1943–
    The hidden injuries of class.
    Bibliography: p.
      1. Labor and laboring classes—United States—1914–
      2. Social classes—United States. 3. Social
conflict. I. Cobb, Jonathan, joint author.
II. Title.
[HD8072.S487 1973]   301.44'42'0973   73–4515
ISBN 0–394–71940–9

For ANGUS CAMERON

CONTENTS

PERSONAL ACKNOWLEDGMENTS

The following people worked as interviewers for this study: Claire Siegel-baum, Petra Szonyi, Nancy Lyons, Quaker Case, Sandra Warren, Guillemette Alperovitz, Robert Manz, Dennis Brown, Stephen Goldin, and John McDermott. All treated their interviews as more than a job, and the people they interviewed as more than informants. Acknowledgment is also abundantly due to the people who worked on transcribing the interviews, a difficult and frustrating task: Patricia Lark, Patti Shockro, Betsey Cobb, and Carol Sennett.

Earlier versions of this book were read by Betsey Cobb, Susanna Cobb, Jon Livingston, Thomas Engelhardt, Nancy Lyons, John Case, Elliott Sclar, Claire Siegelbaum, Richard Locke, S. M. Miller, Stephan Thernstrom, Patricia and Brendan Sexton, and Herbert Gans.

In 1968, when we conceived the idea for this study, most of the foundations we approached thought about workers, if they thought about them at all, as a "problem," a problem embodied in the Wallace movement. We thank Thomas Cooney at the Ford Foundation for taking a larger interest; in our subsequent dealings with Shirley Teper, Basil Whiting, and Mitchell Sviridoff we received in full the gifts a foundation has to confer: money, encouragement, and complete freedom to go our own way.

The text was strengthened at a critical stage of the writing by three editors at Alfred A. Knopf: Melvin Rosenthal, Daniel Okrent, and Angus Cameron. Angus Cameron, in particular, has stayed with this book through all its trials, yet remained its most disinterested critic.

FOREWORD

This book was written by Richard Sennett, but results from a collaboration between Richard Sennett and Jonathan Cobb extending across the past four years. The ideas in this book come from that collaboration, so that while Sennett is the writer of the present text, he is not its sole author. It is also true that setting words on paper is so personal a task that no two people will express shared ideas the same way; the emphasis and emotional tone of this book are Sennett's own. For these reasons the editorial "we" has been used. Jonathan Cobb has written an Afterword that gives another emphasis to the same research materials.

The book comes out of a project financed by the Ford Foundation which Richard Sennett directed during its initial phase and Jonathan Cobb during its final phase.

INTRODUCTION

HIDDEN INJURIES

INTRODUCTION

Two labor organizers, formed in the crucible of the Great Depression, once communists now socialists without a home, sit in a room arguing about what went wrong. They are friends of Richard Sennett; they are thirty years older than he; they argue with a passion that at the time—it is 1961—he cannot understand. They argue about why the workers in America have not become a revolutionary force.

"I remember 1937 and '38 so well," Arnold says, "how much hope I had. The auto strike seemed to make people see the light; when I went into a community I didn't have to explain there was a class struggle. No doctrine. The struggle was in the men. It seemed, you know, natural to commit yourself to the class struggle then, because you felt ten, fifteen years there would be an uprising here like in Russia."

"But you quit the Party because of the trials in Russia, no?" Sidney asks. "The workers didn't fail you, the Party did, right?"

"The thing about Sidney," Arnold says, turning to his host, "is that the worker is like a virgin to him. Make the wrong approach to her, rape her, like the Party did, she goes crazy; make the right approach, she wants it, and you live happily ever after . . . Lookit, Sidney, you got to admit this. Your union has got more money for its men than most, good benefits, all that shit. So you're going to figure out a new approach to explaining the class struggle, they're going to vote you out of office, because they'll be the ones to lose."

It is 1971. Both Arnold and Sidney have left their unions. Ironically, Arnold the "realist" about how much you can expect from workers has been voted out; Sidney the idealist has resigned to go into business. They are both victims, members of a generation of radicals sacrificed, as one writer has put it, to a god that failed—Sidney feeling betrayed by revolutionary communism, Arnold by the workers. It is 1971. In the United States there have occurred both white backlash and the most turbulent rejection of organized union authority among young workers; in France, where workers in 1968 had not fully responded to the pleas of young students to make revolution together, wildcat strikes and factory revolts are now everywhere in the industrial suburbs around Paris; Italy is on the verge of democratically electing a communist government whose leaders are devout Catholics. Radical intellectuals are still fighting about the issues that wrecked Arnold and Sidney's lives.

In *Condemned to Freedom*, William Pfaff echoes Arnold's disillusionment with workers as revolutionaries. "Once the worker has won a position of basic economic security and reasonable expectations," he writes, "he has considerably more reason to be conservative on social issues than the

4

middle-class executive or professional man. . . . For the workingman, everything could be jeopardized by radical change." The argument is straightforward and rather brutal: human beings can be bought off from humanitarian concerns; the present system of affluence has bought off the worker.

The views of someone who has kept Sidney's faith in working-class struggle are more complicated. Recently John Gerassi published an interview he conducted with the French philosopher Jean Paul Sartre. In the wake of the events of 1968 Sartre regards himself as having moved from the position of an *intellectuel de gauche* (an intellectual of leftist persuasion) to that of an *intellectuel gauchiste* (a leftist of intellectual background and training); he now supports all sorts of Maoist and other revolutionary movements to the left of the established and rather staid French Communist Party. The Party has betrayed the workers, Sartre believes, by speaking an intellectual language irrelevant to their experience. Such established communist papers as *Rouge* argue about dialectical principles and the Gospel according to Saint Marx. Why should workers care about such things?

What then is the role of the *intellectuel gauchiste?*, Gerassi asks Sartre, and the philosopher gives a peculiar answer. The only writing now worth doing, he says, is the political tract, because the position of the intellectual has changed: "He must now write *with* the masses, and through them, therefore put his technical knowledge at their disposal. In other words, his privileged status is over. Today it is sheer bad faith, hence counterrevolutionary, for the intellectual to dwell on his own problems." Sartre now believes the intellectual must sacrifice himself for the workers. "He must be dedicated to work for their problems, not his own."

Yet, Gerassi points out, Sartre has just finished a two-thousand-page book on the novelist Flaubert. Why? Sartre accuses himself in reply: "My book on Flaubert may, indeed, be a form of petty-bourgeois escapism." Again, he has criticized the Castro regime in Cuba for its treatment of Heberto Padilla, a poet jailed for alleged counterrevolutionary attitudes. All genuinely revolutionary governments, Sartre says, must honor creative freedom. But, Gerassi asks, isn't that precisely to put the intellectual in a special position?

In his guilty confusion, Sartre shows himself to share, at least implicitly, two assumptions about workers with the ex-trade unionist Arnold and with William Pfaff. First, that the man of culture—the poet, philosopher, social visionary—inhabits a world that cannot be assimilated to the realities of working-class life. Sartre apologizes for thinking about Flaubert. He respects the work workers do, indeed he idolizes it; he is afraid he will alienate them by *his* work. Yet at the same time he is afraid his work is innately privileged, and that men of culture like Padilla may have certain rights against the revolution. Pfaff and Arnold believe workers will never make a revolution because their position in society prevents their attaining a vision of Justice and Right such as men of culture can see. In both cases, culture and the masses, if not necessarily enemies, have at best few interests in common.

Second, Arnold and Pfaff think the conservatism of workers is a logical one. Both of them assume that workers have in the last two or three decades made enough money, acquired enough possessions, achieved so much in comparison to the physical degradation of the Great Depression years, that the workers want to protect what they have and the system that has made these triumphs possible.

Sidney and Sartre accept the logic, but not the conclusion, of this argument. The worker has not really gotten his fair share in the society, both say; if only he can be made to see how he has been used, he will rise up and rebel. In polemics against the myth of affluent workers, many other social critics take up the same ground: a working-class politics is possible now because workers are in fact denied equity in the social system. The basis of rebellion, however, is still a calculation of material interest. Material hardship caused by the system makes people rebel, material reward makes them defend. That is to say, none of these men, on either side of the argument, really believes that the aphorism, *Man lives not by bread alone,* applies to workers.

People have thought for a long time, of course, that artists, writers, and others of high culture need more than bread; the Romantic movement of the early nineteenth century took fire out of the image of the artist or writer as a person driven by something greater than the desire to survive comfortably—the artist or writer, but not the general run of men. The calculus of material well-being to which both sides of this debate subscribe hinges on an historic assumption that between the world of culture and the realities of life for the masses there is an unbridgeable gulf.

When men like Sartre or Sidney expound a politics of working-class revolt based principally on material deprivation, they are, despite their best intentions, entering conservative enemy territory, where such thinkers as Tocqueville, Nietzsche, and Ortega y Gasset hold sway. These men all proclaimed mass politics to be based on calculations of mass interests, and condemned the masses for it. The "humanity" of these conservatives rested on their declaration that they, and the few other men of culture alienated from the masses, must conduct their lives on nonmaterialistic principles of self-sacrifice to an ideal, a repudiation of concern for security, a demand for civility which is not the same as a demand for fraternity. Let us be realistic, they, like Arnold and Pfaff, have said; such commitments demand too much of most people. To have culture you must have an elite.

We must apologize for the harsh tone of these beginning remarks. The genuine commitment of Jean Paul Sartre or of laborites like Sidney we no more question than we do the disillusioned sincerity of Arnold and of William Pfaff. But the hidden, condescending consensus among these seeming opponents, bred of a long-standing tradition that divorces culture from society, is necessary for you to see, if you are to understand the experience which led the authors to undertake this book. For both of us unknowingly shared these assumptions when we began, thinking at first that we occupied conflicting sides in the debate typified by Arnold and Sidney.

Richard Sennett grew up in the Middle West, attending a military and then public schools. The adult world he knew had passed through the political storms of the 1930's with some of its members wounded, some crushed. He came to believe that a revolution is necessary, but that the workers of America have been too thoroughly integrated into its riches to make the revolution.

Jonathan Cobb grew up in a well-to-do New England

family. His politics are not an inheritance, but of his own making. Cobb came of age conscious of his own privileged isolation, and with a conviction of, as Sartre puts it, "a terrible, unseen denial" among manual laborers, an inequity in the lives of people he had never known. He came to believe in a working-class politics coupled with a sense of estrangement from the upper-class environment into which he was born.

We are not replicas of Arnold and Sidney, because our points of view up to a few years ago were not the product of any personal involvement in the lives of workingpeople. The more we talked with each other, the more our differences were expressed and ambivalences explored, the more it seemed we ought to create that involvement. Since neither of us is adept at practical affairs, and since it would have seemed a presumptuous beginning, we could not repeat Sidney and Arnold's experience of "organizing" workers who were strangers. What we could do is talk. One of us by professional training, both by personal temperament, leaned to intensive and probing conversations as the best way to get a sense of what the distance we have referred to was all about. We hoped to learn what issues now engage a group of American manual laborers and their families that bear on this classic division between culture and the masses of society.

Having defined, perhaps too clearly, our vague purposes at the start of our work, we must explain why this book has become more than a report on a series of conversations. As a result of those conversations, we have come to see that both sides in the argument about workers, rebellion, and culture think more simplistically about workers than workers think about themselves. The complexity of working-class consciousness demands of the listener a fresh theory to explain what he is hearing, a theory that, in this book, involves speculation and generalization far beyond the boundaries of the conversations themselves.

To begin at the beginning, it is necessary to see the peculiarly American connotations of the idea of an isolated working class. Pfaff and Sartre, as we have said, posit an isolation of workingpeople from the issues that dominate the lives of men of high culture; in the United States, however, the majority of white urban workers have faced an historic isolation rooted in seemingly different, though in fact related, causes.

In the manufacturing cities of Western Europe during the nineteenth century, children of the countryside became the proletariat. The worker who was bred in city ways and comfortable in its crowds could indeed be found in the factories, but he did not dominate them. Even in England, where urban centers had been home to the new industrial order for generations, the working classes of Manchester or Birmingham were swelled each decade principally by people who could remember another way of life. Though Saint-Simon or Marx could speak of the "industrial era" as a fact taken for granted, less than a hundred years ago most people still had experience of rhythms of labor tied to the change of seasons, with diversity in human affairs measured by the boundaries of a village.

The rural influx to cities was not, four or five generations ago, a simple affair. People moved in complicated ways, often migrating in a chain from small farm to small town, then from town to cities of increasingly larger size. In Europe, a rural crisis forced vast population movements during the last decades of the nineteenth century. Large landholders no longer found it profitable to keep peasants on their land; small farmers could no longer survive in an agricultural market swayed by international trade; local craftsmen could not compete with the cheaper commodities of factory production. The rhythms of rural life were disrupted by the magnet of the city, whose rulers capitalized on the disaffection of the rural young to draw in a supply of labor. More overt upheavals occurred through the persecution of minorities in villages, such as the Jews in Lithuania.

The American workers in cities of the Midwest and East Coast are predominantly men with this past. The majority of the 35 million white manual laborers in these cities have come from Ireland and Southern and Eastern Europe during the last four generations, and the chaos of the old country has cast a shadow across generations of these Americans still called "ethnics." It has commonly been thought that the settlement of Italians, Poles, or Greeks in little enclaves in American cities, in neighborhoods where the old language was spoken and the old customs kept, embodied a preservation of what the immigrant had known in his native land. But it is perhaps more accurate to say that these veterans of European turmoil found in the strange and alien cities of America a way to re-ignite some feeling of common custom and culture that had been disintegrating at home. "In the desert of America," a Russian Jew remarked in the 1920's, "it is easier to remain Russian in the old ways than among the iron mills in the Urals."

Yet this national crisis in the old country is not a sufficient explanation for the historic isolation of such ethnic groups. For this isolation also resulted from the impact these immigrants had on the economic life of the growing American cities.

Before the arrival of large numbers of immigrants, labor for industrial production was scarce, and machines were used in a special way to counteract the lack of sufficient urban workmen; machines were constructed to replace, wherever possible, *unskilled* labor, thus freeing scarce manpower for the jobs involving more skill, judgment, and complexity. When human labor was replaced by machines, as happened to the Lowell or Waltham mill girls, it occurred where workers performed unskilled tasks. The cost of unskilled human toil was greater than the cost of running machines.°

The influx of large numbers of destitute Europeans at the century's end changed this economic relationship. For example, Polish immigrants, looking desperately for work— any kind of work at any wage—arriving in the steel towns of western Pennsylvania, presented the region's industrialists with a substantial pool of cheap labor that would cost less to employ than the then-existing machines. Industrialists thereupon began to use machines to replace *skilled* labor in a situation where unskilled, unorganized labor was abundant.† In other words, this immigrant influx came to pose a serious, though indirect, threat to the jobs of established skilled workers—not only in steel, but in carriage-making, in printing, in

° H. J. Habakkuk, *American & British Technology in the 19th Century* (Cambridge U. Press; n.d.) is an interesting discussion.

† David Brody, *Steelworkers in America: The Nonunion Era* (Russell; 1969).

textiles. And, not surprisingly, a deep hostility arose among the old Americans toward the newcomers.

The "social consciousness" of the new migrant was fixed on the problems he had left behind at home. In entering on the new experience of working for wages, he was concerned, beyond his own survival, with sending money back to relatives in the old country so that they could join him in the New World or survive the rural economic disaster in Europe.° The idea of formal labor organization was unknown to most of the immigrants. The ever-growing supply of unskilled labor made it almost impossible to organize stable industrial unions even when the idea was advanced— the skilled-crafts workers were, of course, uninterested in uniting with unskilled foreigners. Indeed, employers used the threat of being reduced to the level of the immigrants to tame skilled-labor agitation. If the skilled worker was obedient and did not organize, employers offered him the hope of at least semiskilled work, as machines took away his old job.

Although in the twentieth century skilled labor has reasserted itself, this traumatic shift to a higher technology at the end of the last century established a native source of isolation for the urban immigrant of four generations ago: he came to the American factory at a moment when his presence allowed the growth of a new technology destructive to already-established workers. The hostilities sparked under these conditions left him only his countrymen for support.

It was perhaps no accident that a second force isolating the immigrant came into play at the same time. By the turn

° Oscar Handlin, *The Uprooted* (Grosset & Dunlap; 1957); *The Americans: A New History of the People of the United States* (Atlantic Monthly Press; 1963).

of the century, attitudes had crystallized toward foreigners whose closest equivalent is what we call today racism. These attitudes produced a kind of moral hierarchy of national and cultural differences in which the Western Europeans—with the exception of the Irish—stood at the top, diligent, hard-working, and for the most part, skilled laborers, and in which Slavs, Bohemians, Jews, and Southern Europeans stood lower, accused of dirtiness, secretiveness, or laziness. It is at this time that the image of the non-Teutonic or non-British immigrant as a potential criminal, at worst inclined to bomb-throwing and anarchism, but in any case brutish, surfaces in American folk mythology. Together with the schisms the immigrant brought from his own past, and the economic hostility he encountered at the factory from established labor, national stereotypes forced the ethnic worker to turn to people like himself for comfort and warmth, in little Italys and little Polands hostile to outsiders, "urban villages" stretching over time from the end of the nineteenth century to the middle of our own.°

It was into this inward-turning urban world that most of the people we interviewed in Boston were born. Within its boundaries, people preserved a sociability little known on the outside. Its focus was the street. Almost all of the middle-aged adults with whom we spoke remembered their childhood scenes as street scenes—family scenes, too, for their parents were there, shopping, talking to neighbors, sitting on stoops after the evening meal. Boston children growing up in the 1930's and '40's were planted in the midst

° For a discussion of ethnic neighborhoods as "urban villages," see Herbert Gans, *The Urban Villagers* (Free Press; 1962).

of an especially vivid ethnic life, strong traces of which have survived. On Friday and Saturday, an open-air market still envelops the Italian section, where old men bargain hard and seldom in English; in South Boston, people still celebrate the Irish national holidays with fervor, and old men there who have never been to Ireland talk with Irish brogues.

Historians and sociologists have asked themselves repeatedly why the urban villages have lasted so long. A number of years ago, Nathan Glazer and Daniel P. Moynihan argued° that there is group will and choice embodied in this ethnic isolation, apart from economic tensions and turmoil in the mother countries. Ethnicity, they said, is a way of preserving some special identity in the midst of an American mass, a way of maintaining distinctive traditions and rituals even after a person has the practical opportunity to "melt" into "average" Americanness. Many observers have since taken issue with this thesis, arguing that isolation was in fact beyond the control of immigrant groups. Why do you talk about choice, they have said to Glazer and Moynihan, when the whole history of urban ethnic groups in American society shows an isolation bred of economic rejection in the old country and in the new? Father Andrew Greeley remarks, for instance, that although many people from ethnic backgrounds have made dramatic economic changes in their lives, the ethnic heritage that stays with them most powerfully is the memory of group traditions practiced in poverty in the teeth of a hostile native American culture.

This debate has given way to another. The urban villages

° In *Beyond the Melting Pot* (MIT Press; 1958).

which withstood native prejudice, the hostility of skilled native workers, and the economic shocks of the Great Depression have in recent years been subjected to a new set of forces, thrusting people into problems beyond the power of the old historic institutions to meet.

The urban "renewal" of central cities has been the most striking intrusion on the isolation of urban Americans of recent ethnic origins. The urban villages are often situated in areas where the housing is old, worn, and close to the central business district, and they have become prime targets for planners who dream of rivers of concrete connecting the office with the suburban bedroom, or of towers of glass as symbols of rebirth for the metropolitan economic order.

These communities have also been forcefully integrated into the larger society by national problems that are too powerful to be excluded. "Yes, you might call me an 'Italian-American,'" one woman remarked to us, "but it doesn't do me much good when I have to face my kids taking drugs." Inflation in rents and prices often forces people to move away from their old neighborhoods, as does the fear of crime.

Displacements caused by urban renewal often leave the uprooted with a sense of "grieving" akin to what they have felt when a member of the family has died, a grieving accentuated by the fact that they personally or their political representatives have been largely defeated in fights to stop "progress." ° The fears of drugs and crime are similarly joined to a feeling that neither the individual nor the tradi-

° Marc Fried, "Grieving for a Lost Home," in Leonard J. Duhl, ed., *The Urban Condition* (New York: Basic Books; 1963). Gordon Fellman, manuscript on highway protest, in preparation.

tional institutions of the ethnic culture—the family, the Church, the local politicians—have much power to resist these threats.

One way to interpret this forced integration is that it is leading the mass of America's white laborers to become "workers" in the classic sense of the term. With the cultural shelter of the ethnic community crumbling—so this view runs—ethnic workers are now coming to grips with their true position in American capitalism: they are powerless in the hands of the economic and political forces controlling the cities. The wave of working-class protest in recent years would then appear as a groping to find a political voice as workers, rather than as Irishmen or Poles, a search that at first errs in choosing the wrong targets, like Blacks or radical students, for its anger.

This interpretation of the historical shifts in the experience of urban ethnic workers falls back on a calculus of material well-being; it prophesies a new, rebellious class consciousness arising from the shock American white workers are undergoing, as they are forced beyond the ethnic village into deprivations caused by living just as workers.

Critics following the logic of Arnold or Pfaff, on the other hand, can see in the breakup of the ethnic village support for their own pessimism. Herbert Gans argues, for example, that the ethnic enclaves have fragmented at least in part by the voluntary desire of their inhabitants: as families make economic and occupational gains, they move out to the suburbs to join the ranks of the middle class. Much of the discontent voiced in the last few years by white workers, this view holds, is precisely against those who challenge the system. The historic changes in the lives of American blue-collar ethnics, on this account too, rest on a calculus of material self-interest.

In our own work, we began to see from the first interview on that urban laborers themselves, no less than their critics, are aware of the momentous change in their lives the decline of the old neighborhoods has caused; these working-people of Boston are trying to find out what position they occupy in America as a whole. To create images of their place, however, they use a language more complicated, more puzzling, than the computations of material well-being their interpreters use. For the people we interviewed, integration into American life meant integration into a world with different symbols of human respect and courtesy, a world in which human capabilities are measured in terms profoundly alien to those that prevailed in the ethnic enclaves of their childhood. The changes in their lives mean more to them than a chance, or a failure, to acquire middle-class *things*. For them, history is challenging them and their children to become "cultured," in the intellectual's sense of that word, if they want to achieve respect in the new American terms; and toward that challenge they feel deeply ambivalent. Perhaps the best way to illustrate this ambivalence is to describe what occurred in our first interview.

Frank Rissarro,° a third-generation Italian-American, forty-four years old when we talked with him, had worked his way up from being a shoeshine boy at the age of nine to

° This is not his real name, nor are the details that follow about his job, age, and income precisely accurate. Our method of disguising identities to protect anonymity is more fully explained at the end of this chapter.

classifying loan applications in a bank. He makes $10,000 a year, owns a suburban home, and every August rents a small cottage in the country. He is a man who at first glance appears satisfied—"I know I did a good job in my life"—and yet he is also a man who feels defensive about his honor, fearing that people secretly do not respect him; he feels threatened by his children, who are "turning out just the way I want them to be," and he runs his home in a dictatorial manner.

Rissarro was born in 1925, the second-eldest child and only son of parents who lived in a predominantly Italian section of Boston. His father, an uneducated day laborer, worked hard, drank hard, and beat his wife and children often. As a young boy, Rissarro was not interested in school —his life was passed in constant fear of his father's violence. He was regarded by his family as a spoiled brat, with no brains and no common sense. His sisters and cousins did better than he scholastically, all finishing high school. Yet even as a child, Rissarro worked nights and weekends helping to support his family. At sixteen he quit school, feeling incapable of doing the work and out of place. After two years in the military, he worked as a meat-cutter for nearly twenty years.

Rissarro was and is a man of ambition. The affluence spreading across America in the decades following the Second World War made him restless—he wanted to either get a butcher shop of his own or get out. The capital for a small business being beyond his reach, he had a friend introduce him to the branch manager of a bank setting up a new office in his neighborhood. He won a job processing loans for people who come in off the street; he helps them fill out the forms, though he is still too low-level to have the power to approve or disapprove the loans themselves.

A success story: from chaos in the Depression, from twenty years of hacking away at sides of beef, Rissarro now wears a suit to work and has a stable home in respectable surroundings. Yes, it is a success story—except that *he* does not read it that way.

As we explored with Rissarro the reasons why these good things have come to him, we found the declarations of self-satisfaction almost instantly giving way to a view of himself as a passive agent in his own life, a man who has been on the receiving end of events rather than their cause: "I was just at the right place at the right time," he says again and again. "I was lucky," he claims, in describing how he emotionally withstood the terrors of his father's home.

Is this modesty? Not for him. He feels passive in the midst of his success because he feels illegitimate, a pushy intruder, in his entrance to the middle-class world of neat suburban lawns, peaceable families, happy friendships. Despite the fact that he has gained entrée, he doesn't believe he deserves to be respected. In discussing, for instance, his marriage—to a woman somewhat more educated than he, from an Italian background equivalent to "lace-curtain Irish"—Rissarro told us something impossible to believe, considering his ungrammatical speech, his obsession with his childhood, his mannerisms and gestures: "My wife didn't know that I had no background to speak of, or else she would never have married me." The possibility that she accepted him for himself, and never made an issue of where he came from, he simply cannot accept.

Sociologists have a neat formula to explain the discontent

caused by upward mobility; they call Frank's malaise a product of "status incongruity": Because Frank does not yet know the rules of his new position, because he is caught between two worlds, he feels something is wrong with him. This formula falls back on an image of the antithesis between working-class struggle and educated, "higher" culture.

The trouble here, however, is that Frank *doesn't* feel caught between two worlds. He knows what the rules of middle-class life are, he has played at them now for some years; furthermore, he is not in any way ashamed of his working-class past. Indeed, he is proud of it, he thinks it makes him a more honest person at work:

"I'm working, like I said, with fellows that are educated, college boys, in that office. I'm about the only one in there in any straits to say I'm educated. I'm enjoying this job, I'm going in with the big shots. I go in at nine, I come out at five. *The other fellows, because they got an education, sneaks out early and comes in late.* The boss knows I'm there, a reliable worker. 'Cause I've had the factory life, I know what it is. I mean, a man deserves—the least you can do is put your hours in and do your job. I'm a good employee. I know I am because I see others who are educated."

In fact, toward educated white-collar work itself, beyond all its symbolic connotations of success, Frank Rissarro harbors an innate disrespect: "These jobs aren't real work where you make something—it's just pushing papers."

Then why has he striven so hard to be upwardly mobile? One ready answer is that he wanted the house, the suit, the cottage in the country. And Rissarro himself gives that answer at first. After a few hours of talk, however, he conveys a more complicated and difficult set of feelings.

The poverty of his childhood he speaks about as something shameful, not because there was a lack of things, but rather because the people who had nothing acted like animals. He remembers this particularly in terms of his father —his father's poverty and his drunken brutality toward Frank and Frank's mother are interwoven in Frank's memory. Other images in his conversation concerning the poor, both white and black, similarly fuse material deprivation with chaotic, arbitrary, and unpredictable behavior; he sees poverty, in other words, as depriving men of the capacity to act rationally, to exercise self-control. A poor man, therefore, *has* to want upward mobility in order to establish dignity in his own life, and dignity means, specifically, moving toward a position in which he deals with the world in some controlled, emotionally restrained way. People who have been educated, on the other hand, are supposed to already possess this capacity. They are supposed to have developed skills for taming the world without force or passion.

Frank feels that it is such people on whom he ought to model the changes he wants in his own life. And yet, paradoxically, he doesn't respect the content of their powers: just as intellect gives a man respect in the world, the educated do nothing worth respecting; their status means they can cheat. In a further twist, Rissarro then proceeds to turn the paradox into a terrible accusation against himself: "As far as I'm concerned, I got through life by always trying to depend on the other guy to do my work. But when it came to my hands, I could do all the work myself."

Capturing respect in the larger America, then, means to

Frank getting into an educated position; but capturing that respect means that he no longer respects himself. This contradiction ran through every discussion we held, as an image either of what people felt compelled to do with their own lives or of what they sought for their sons. If the boys could get educated, anybody in America would respect them; and yet, as we shall see, the fathers felt education would lead the young into work not as "real" as their own.

A workingman looks at the privileges high culture bestows in much the same light as does Ortega y Gasset or William Pfaff—that high culture permits a life in which material need can be transcended by a higher form of self-control; he looks at the claims of intellectual privilege, however, with the same jaundiced eyes as does Sartre. On this ground, the workingman's feelings about his leaving the isolated, poor ethnic community have the same ambivalence that the radical intellectual experiences when he seeks to define his place in relation to the workingman.

Yet, why should Frank Rissarro be worrying about his legitimacy? And why has he chosen as a "prestige model" a kind of work activity he despises?

This paradox might, of course, be read simply as a conflict in the individual personalities of men like Frank Rissarro. It is more accurate, however, to see it as an issue introduced into their lives by the America outside the urban village. The story these workingmen have to tell is not just who they are but what are the contradictory codes of respect in the America of their generation.

How Frank Rissarro talked to his interviewer provides some beginning clues in this regard.

· · ·

The Hidden Injuries of Class

Frank Rissarro did not so much grant an interview as give a confession. The interviewer began by asking a neutral question, something about what Rissarro remembered of Boston while he was growing up. He replied by talking with little interruption for more than three hours about intimate feelings and experiences to this stranger whom he had never met before. Rissarro talked to the interviewer in a peculiar way: he treated him as an emissary from a different way of life, as a representative of a higher, more educated class, before whom he spread a justification of his entire life. At various points where he spoke of situations where he felt powerless and the interviewer sympathized, Rissarro would suddenly respond to him as simply a human being, not as an emissary sent in judgment; but then, as he returned to the story of his life, which he seemed to live through again as he described it, the interviewer once again became a representative of a class of people who could do what they wanted and who made him feel inadequate. It was Rissarro's chief concern throughout to show why circumstances had not permitted him to take charge of his life in the same way.

Yet this man is someone who feels he has done a good job in establishing a stable family and margin of security in contrast to the life of poverty and turmoil he knew as a child during the Depression. Why then is he so defensive?

The word "educated" as used by Rissarro, and by other men and women we talked to, is what psychologists call a "cover term"; that is, it stands for a whole range of experiences and feelings that may in fact have little to do with formal schooling. Education covers, at the most abstract level, the development of capacities within a human being. At the most concrete level, education meant to the people we interviewed getting certificates for social mobility and job choice, and they felt that American society parcels out the certificates very unequally and unfairly, so that middle-class people have more of a chance to become educated than themselves. But if the abstract is connected to the concrete, this means middle-class people have more of a chance than workers to escape from becoming creatures of circumstance, more chance to develop the defenses, the tools of personal, rational control that "education" gives. Why should one class of human beings get a chance to develop the weapons of self more than another? And yet, if that class difference is a *fait accompli*, what has a man without education got inside himself to defend against this superior power?

Rissarro believes people of a higher class have a power to judge him because they seem internally more developed human beings; and he is afraid, because they are better armed, that they will not respect him. He feels compelled to justify his own position, and in his life he has felt compelled to put himself up on their level in order to earn respect. All of this, in turn—when he thinks just of himself and *is not comparing himself* to his image of people in a higher class—all of this is set against a revulsion against the work of educated people in the bank, and a feeling that manual labor has more dignity.

What does he make of this contradiction in his life? That he is an impostor—but more, that the sheer fact that he is troubled must prove he really is inadequate. After all, he has played by the rules, he has gained the outward signs of material respectability; if, then, he still feels defenseless, something must be wrong with *him:* his unhappiness seems to him a sign that he simply cannot become the kind of person other people can respect.

This tangle of feelings appeared again and again as we talked to people who started life as poor, ethnically isolated laboring families, and have been successful in making the sort of material gains that are supposed to "melt" people into the American middle class.

The children who get formal education are no more exempt than parents like Rissarro from a feeling of inadequate defenses in the very midst of success. Nationally, about half the children from white, blue-collar homes get started in the kind of schooling their parents want—that is, about half go beyond high school. There is a large difference between girls and boys in this; depending on whose figures you use, between ten and twenty-five percent of boys from blue-collar homes receive some further schooling, while between forty and fifty percent of the girls do. A much smaller percentage of boys gets through four years of college or technical school (three to five percent); a slightly higher, though still small, percentage of girls do.

As with blue-collar workers who have moved into offices, we are dealing with a minority—a minority, however, on whom much hope is pinned. Observers of the college scene like John McDermott have suggested that this may be a more desperately unhappy group of students than the disaffected young from suburban homes.* McDermott and, in another context, David Riesman believe these working-class boys and girls are made to feel inadequate by a "laying-on of culture" practiced in college by their teachers and the

* See John McDermott, "The Laying On of Culture," *The Nation*, vol. 208, no. 10 (March 10, 1969).

more privileged students—a process that causes people to feel inadequate in the same way "status incongruity" does, by subjecting them to an unfamiliar set of rules in a game where respect is the prize.

Yet here is James, in his third year at a local college accessible to sons and daughters from blue-collar homes. James's father works as a clerk for the city by day and mends rugs at night and on the weekend. James knows the rules for making it in college, and he has survived the weeding-out process of the first years with good grades. But James disrespects school in the same way Frank disrespects pushing papers around at the bank; the status of "educated man" is greater than that of a craftsman, but the intrinsic satisfaction seems less. James feels, however, that he must stay in school, above all for his father's sake:

"The American Dream for my father is to see his kids get a college education, something he never had. If it had to kill them, they were gonna get a college education. He never really forced it on us, but we knew that this was really gonna make him happy—that we could get a college degree."

James also knows what leaving school would mean materially: a loss of security, status jobs, money. He is going to stay in school, because he feels compelled by these material considerations even as he disrespects them on their own.

How does he deal with the conflict success in school has set up in his life? Like Frank Rissarro, he blames himself for feeling so ambivalent. On the one hand he says, "I still don't have the balls to go out into the world," i.e., to quit school; on the other hand, "If I really had what it takes, I could make this school thing worthwhile." He takes personal responsibility for his social position, and the result is that he makes himself feel inadequate no matter which way he turns in attempting to deal with success.

James has gone through a profound dislocation in his life, and his discontent is pronounced. His problem, however, is shared in more muted form by others who have made more modest gains. These are kids who have had a little schooling beyond high school and then gone into such jobs as sales-work or management traineeships. They feel they have had more opportunity open to them than their manual-laboring parents. At the same time, they see the parents' work as intrinsically more interesting and worthwhile, and they suffer, therefore, from a feeling of not having made use of their opportunities. When all the discipline of sticking it out in school yields an occupation they feel little engagement in, they hold themselves to blame, for not feeling more self-confidence, for having failed to develop. "If only I had what it takes," says a young shoe salesman, son of a factory laborer, "things would have been different."

One way to make sense of these confusing metaphors of self-worth is to recast them as issues of *freedom* and *dignity*. Class is a system for limiting freedom: it limits the freedom of the powerful in dealing with other people, because the strong are constricted within the circle of action that maintains their power; class constricts the weak more obviously in that they must obey commands. What happens to the dignity men see in themselves and in each other, when their freedom is checked by class?

In England or France today, one would have to give a different reply to this general question than one would in the United States. In cultures with still-strong working-class traditions, or a sense of working-class solidarity, the respect as equals that workingmen may not get from those who command them they can get from each other. Richard Hoggart's *The Uses of Literacy* is a beautiful evocation of the feeling among laborers that we are unfree, but dignified in our oppression because we have each other. In the *faubourgs rouges* around Paris, workers similarly take real pride in their class position.

But if it is possible, then, to feel dignified even as one recognizes that he has less material freedom, fewer work options, less chance of education than others, why is it that in America men like Frank Rissarro feel their dignity is on the line? Why do they take their class position so personally? And especially someone like James, who is actively engaged in self-development, in acquiring the education Rissarro feels he lacks—why does he have a similar feeling of vulnerability?

These are the kinds of questions this book will try to answer. The circumstances of urban workers in America already sketched provide some partial answers: the ethnic refuge is fragmenting as the ethnic turf in the city is being destroyed; both these men have changed classes in a society that, unlike Britain, celebrates the myth of permeation of social classes, and social mobility creates status anxiety. But these circumstantial answers are too simple. That an increase in material power and freedom of choice should be accompanied by a crisis in self-respect deserves more probing study.

It is worth remarking here on the obtuseness of the position advanced by B. F. Skinner in *Beyond Freedom and Dignity*, when his clichés of behavioral psychology are applied to actual human lives. Skinner says that freedom of the individual and his dignity as an autonomous man are unscientific myths; yet here are two human beings, Rissarro and James, reared in a class where men have severe limits imposed on their individual freedom to choose, men struggling to establish more freedom in order to gain dignity—dignity they find hard to define—men whose struggle, while successful on the surface, is eroding their confidence in themselves. What insight do we gain into their actions by calling the search for freedom and dignity a myth, what do we learn about the culture, and why it is so structured that the more it gives them the more it makes them feel vulnerable? Why talk about getting "beyond" the idea of freedom and dignity in individual lives when the society is so arranged that these men have as yet had little taste of either? The argument of the present book will center, like Skinner's, on attacking individualism, but surely it is impossible to understand a social evil merely by dismissing its power to command men's imagination as a matter of "insufficient knowledge" or "prescientific belief."

The one bit of information appearing so far that will be crucial, in fact, for understanding how the struggle for freedom and dignity has become destructive in America is the value men like Frank Rissarro and James put on knowledge. Knowledge through formal education they see as giving a man the tools for achieving freedom—by permitting him to control situations, and by furnishing him with access to a greater set of roles in life. As things actually stand, however, Certified Knowledge does not mean dignity for either of these men; indeed, it is the reverse, it is a sham. What needs to be understood is how the class structure in America is organized so that *the tools of freedom become sources of indignity.*

Since the life histories presented thus far touch on the issue of social mobility, one moral might be that people are happier if they don't try to push themselves. Perhaps class change in America is such a viciously destructive process that, no matter how it works psychologically, "melting" into the middle classes is not what people from the disintegrating urban villages should do with their lives. The problem with this idea is that the same issues of dignity and self-respect appear in the lives of people who remain manual laborers. These issues concern the everyday experiences of working-class survival as well as the exceptional issues of success.

In our discussions we came across a way of remembering the Depression that appears also in the records Studs Terkel gathered in *Hard Times* and in academic work done by E. Wight Bakke. For workers now fairly secure in their jobs, the Great Depression is remembered as a social disaster that disrupted lives, but so cataclysmic, so out of the power of the individual to control, that all a man could do was struggle to survive the best he could. If he was wiped out, or his fortunes declined, how could he blame himself?

In the economic squeeze workers have felt in recent years, a squeeze much less cataclysmic, one hears running through many conversations about economic woes a kind of defensiveness, a fear that outsiders might blame the worker himself for his economic troubles. This appears, for example, in the following discussion of the repossession of a car:

HUSBAND: So you see, there's nothing we can do about it, I mean it's just a fact of life.

WIFE: That's right, we had a tight margin of maybe ten, fifteen dollars a month beyond the essentials; the bank treated us like criminals for missing the payments during Joe's layoff, they had no right to treat us that way, don't you think?

HUSBAND: It's what burned me, the treatment, you know; I mean, I can get to work without the car, but nobody should get this kind of treatment in America.

The sense of injured dignity here is quite different from the way the husband speaks of his family's losing their house to a bank during the Depression: "Jesus, we just walked out of there and onto the street thinking, 'This ain't happening to us'"; or from reports Terkel gathered like the following:

> I remember a very sinking feeling during the time of the Bank Holiday. I walked down to the corner to buy a paper, giving the man a fifty cents coin. He flipped it up in the air and said, "This is no good" and then threw it in the middle of the street. (Laughs) Some took the Holiday as a huge joke. Others had hysteria, like this newsboy: there isn't any money, there isn't anything. Most people took it calmly. It couldn't get much worse. . . .*

Almost every middle-aged person with whom we spoke believes he is much better off than his parents were, not just during the Depression, but before and after it: "My dad worked like a slave, six days a week; he broke his balls for us kids, and thank God Julie and I don't have to live like that any more." Or: "For the worker, the 'good old days' weren't

* Studs Terkel, *Hard Times* (Pantheon; 1970), p. 423.

so hot; we're damn lucky we don't have to see them again."
Yet these same workers say later, "I think things are bad
now, not just the taxes, you know what I mean, but like the
common man doesn't have too much opportunity," or "I've
had it up to here, there's only so much you can do, and I've
done it, and things are still tight."

Such complaints cover over a deeper fear:

"Well, look, I got three kids now, right, I got to put
money away for their schooling and all, like I don't want to
let them down, I mean, I won't be holding up my end if I
don't work."

"What will my boys think of me if there's no savings for
them to go to college?"

These men's power to stay at work is as much out of their
hands as their fathers' jobs were during the Depression; the
tenure of manual-laboring jobs remains now as in the 1930's
the most sensitive, on the whole, to economic fluctuation.
But the structure of memory in 1970 is this: no one could
blame a father for losing a job during the Depression—but
the more one talks to these men, the more one senses a fear
in each that *he* will be blamed now, *he* will be failing the
others, if he loses his job.°

This fear of being summoned before some hidden bar of
judgment and being found inadequate infects the lives of
people who are coping perfectly well from day to day; it is a
matter of a hidden weight, a hidden anxiety, in the *quality*
of experience, a matter of feeling inadequately in control

° As Bakke points out, urban blue-collar fathers, during the Depression itself,
had similar feelings of personal responsibility for their misfortunes. It is a question
of how people remember the past in an era of greater economic security (E. Wight
Bakke, *The Unemployed Worker* [New Haven: Yale Univ. Press; 1940]).

where an observer making material calculations would conclude the workingman had adequate control.

Carl Dorian is a young electrician apprentice. He is a quiet person, recently married. His life, he feels, has no great drama in it: in trade school he did well enough to know his craft but was not outstanding; outside of school he made friends with a group who still see each other and still all live in the Charlestown district of Boston where they grew up.

"I have no problems, if you know what I mean, but I can't say as I'm really content. There's no problems at work because I just do what the boss says . . . he's not a tyrant or anything; he wants me to do good work, and that's fine, no quarrel with that . . . I can't really figure it out, like I feel impatient sort of . . . No, I like doing electrical work, you get around, you see different kinds of buildings and problems, it's a good way to make a living . . .

"I guess it's a question of, like am I working *for* someone? I . . . I feel like I'm taking shit even when, actually, even when there's nothing wrong . . ."

The interviewer asks him how his feelings come out.

"Well, I hassle the boss about cash . . . I work at union scale, but it's a small business . . . No, I don't mean that, there's other guys I know who do the same thing in big shops . . . See, I feel like I'm being held back, like I'm not on top of things . . . I don't know what you would call it, maybe sort of powerless, but it's a feeling not about any one thing that's gone wrong."

Reports from this country, as well as from France and Italy, tell now of the rebellion of children from laboring homes who have grown up in some security and in some cases prosperity: a willingness to go out on wildcat strikes, against the wishes of their elders in the shops and in the unions, an insistence on immediate wage increases and vacation increases, and disregard of other, traditional issues like sickness benefits, union political work, new plant organizing. Yet this man's feelings cannot be reduced to anger; he wants to "be on top of things," to be in control, and yet he can't pinpoint "any one thing that's gone wrong."

Something about the very discussion of resentment seems to trouble him. "You know, maybe I didn't mean what I said before quite like all that . . . I'm not going to quit, life is all right . . . it's just this feeling at times of not being in control of things that . . . it makes me real intolerant and kind of edgy." Nothing from the familiar vocabulary of visible economic oppression defines his experience: he likes his job, he does it well, his boss is fair.

Carl is looking for some personal control, for a way to feel *he* copes; he uses wage gains from his employer as a weapon in that struggle. But, for a unionized worker, that weapon becomes two-edged. A pipe fitter in Boston who lives next door to a middle-aged schoolteacher makes twice the salary of his neighbor; yet when they meet, the pipe fitter calls the schoolteacher "Mister" and is called in turn by his first name. The schoolteacher thinks of getting rewards from his job internally, in terms of his own individual professional growth. The rewards that appear open to the pipe fitter in the future are *collective* ones, rewards open to all the men in his craft—more money, for instance, more money than the schoolteacher he calls "Mister" can ever hope to see. "What the fuck, I'm going to take the bastards at work for everything I can, but it's not the same thing for Mister Arnold, you know?"

The essential character of money power for most manual workers is that it comes to them not individually, but collectively, through union action. When a labor negotiator sits down to draft a new contract, he does not say to the management that Jones or Smith has done a particularly good job last year, and deserves a raise, he says that X category of labor is worth so much more this year, or that men with X number of years of service are due for a longevity raise, or that X group of workers need a cost-of-living escalator clause. The labor negotiator is fighting for categories of work to be rewarded, not for individuals to be singled out.

Yet the code of respect running through all these people's lives demands that a man "make something of himself," that he justify his material gains by a personal effort. In collective bargaining he is rewarded, if at all, for belonging to a category. Carl's and the pipe fitter's wages have gone up in the last five years, as have their fringe benefits; yet both feel frozen, unable to control their own lives. And it is for this reason that the pipe fitter makes a distinction between himself and Mr. Arnold: the pipe fitter may make more money, but it is Mr. Arnold whose class position appears to hinge on a power inside the man himself.

The rule for respect in America these people read in emerging from their historic isolation is that a man should feel responsibility for his own social position—even if, in a class society, he believes men in general are deprived of the freedom to control their lives.

The people who will appear in this book all feel class and self joined. Those who change class, through a white-collar job or a higher level of education, feel terribly ambivalent about their success, and the ambivalence they treat as a sign of vulnerability in themselves. Those who make reasonably comfortable lives for themselves and their families as workers, who cope without leaving the arena of manual labor, are also touched by the feeling of a powerlessness embedded in the self. This feeling shows in the quality of their day-to-day lives; they hold themselves responsible for the anxiety. Something hidden and perverse is at work in our society so that people lose a conviction of their dignity when they try to take responsibility for either an increase in or a limit on their "freedom" as society defines that word.

There is a telling objection to this definition of the problem: didn't *we*, the interviewers, make these feelings occur? We are upper-middle-class intellectuals talking to workers; naturally we would put them uptight. Despite our best intentions, didn't we make them feel inadequate?

HOW THE CONVERSATIONS IN THIS BOOK CAME TO BE

When we began our talks, these charges seemed depressingly logical. But as we went through more and more interviews, we came to see that this matter of class differences between ourselves and workers is not a personal issue in the sense we first believed. During the course of our interviews, people were reserved with us at first, but when they found our interest was genuine, became personally quite warm. Some kind of trust built up, to the point where people would sometimes invite us to their homes as friends after the talks. The greatest mark of trust we received, however, was when people felt finally free to discuss with us an issue that had long been on their minds about "people like us"; trust was finally established when people felt they could express anger to us about the barriers they felt between people in our class and theirs. "You mean, Dick," a plumber said to Richard Sennett, "you mean you make a good living just by sitting around and thinking? By what right? Now don't take that personally—I mean, I'm sure you're a smart fellow and all that—but that's really the life, not having to break your balls for someone else."

Before the trust developed which permitted people to express anger at the life cultured people had, we were indeed treated as members of a class who made workingmen uneasy. Rissarro's initial apologia is just one example of what that unease did to people as they began to talk about themselves.

In any autobiographical account there occur attempts at self-justification; one sees this in talking with children of twelve as well as with adults. But in these discussions, self-justification took a peculiar form: people felt that an educated, upper-middle-class person was in a position to judge them, and that the judgment rendered would be that working-class people could not be respected as equals; to this fear people responded in one of two ways—either by trying to show that the position they held in society was not personally their fault, or that it was wrong in general for people to make judgments on other people based on social standing. It might seem, then, that, to borrow a phrase from the most class-conscious politician of our time, the emotional impact of the class difference here is a matter of "impudent snobbery," of shaming, of putdown. As perceived by real workers, however, the matter is somewhat more complicated: cultured people do acquire in their eyes a certain right to act as judges of others, because society has put them in a position to develop their insides; on the other hand, it is outrageous for society to do this, because people ought to treat each other as equals. In our interviews, our treatment as members of an educated class reflected the first part of this attitude, and the forging of bonds of personal trust elicited the second. In this way, seeking out the class-consciousness of workers, we found we were going to have to explore our own presence as an active ingredient in the process.

The city of Boston, in which we and the people we interviewed live, is involved in the same sort of relationship. It has harbored—as already noted—a traditionally strong set of ethnic urban villages. In the last decade, however, these villages have severely fragmented; some, like the original Italian community studied by Herbert Gans, have been wholly destroyed by urban renewal. There are relatively few blacks (thirteen percent) in Boston, and the white world surrounding these workingpeople is dominated by what Patricia and Brendan Sexton° call "the New Class"—i.e., people like the interviewers. Highly educated professionals spew forth from the universities in Cambridge, Boston, and Waltham. As the old textile and shoe industries have declined in the Boston area, new industries created by the technological expertise of people from the New Class have provided new forms of manual work—in electronics parts and computer industries in particular. The personal power

° Patricia and Brendan Sexton, *Blue Collars and Hard Hats* (New York: Random House; 1971).

seen in people of the New Class is joined to an economic fact; exertion of this power in the technological field has provided the new lifeblood for factory work in the area.

The casual visitor to Boston is impressed with its age, its slow pace and backward ways in comparison to other American cities, its unusual racial balance for an East Coast city. Were he to drive out of the city center, along Route 128 which rings the city, he would see a kind of clean technological industrial plant which most cities dream of as ideal industry. Indeed, if the Sextons are right that the New Class is becoming the source for more and more of the country's economic growth—a view elaborated by Daniel Bell and Alain Touraine in their theories of post-industrial society— the relationship between manual laborer and New Class member is an important one for the future. The "bias" our presence caused in our interviews, as well as by the peculiar character of the Boston area, was thus at once a limitation and a valuable angle of orientation.

This book grew specifically out of two sources. One was "urban anthropological," in which Richard Sennett acted as participant-observer in communities, in schools, in local clubs and bars; the other was a series of 150 in-depth interviews conducted by both authors between July 1969 and July 1970 with the help of a small staff. We recorded about four hundred hours of discussion, both private interviews and group discussions among workingmen, women, their older children, and ourselves. Two-thirds of the people interviewed formally were in their late thirties or early forties, a very few were grandparents in their sixties, and the rest belonged to a younger generation, in their teens or early twenties. The middle-aged people were largely the third generation in their families to live in America; the younger, the fourth. All of the middle-aged and older men had spent most of their adult lives doing manual work, but at the time we interviewed them some few had moved into low-level white-collar jobs.

In the formal talks, we tried to interview people at our office rather than at their homes, because there were fewer distractions for long sessions, and, as we found, people preferred talking on some neutral ground. The method we evolved was to get a group of people together for a joint discussion and then follow this up with individual interviews. We told people we were preparing a book about workers in the city, and asked if they would help. We never offered to pay them for their time—and we were never asked. We used a tape recorder, which sometimes made people nervous for the first ten minutes or so, but they soon forgot it was there. Occasionally after a group interview, people would stay and listen to the tape and then talk some more.

We had no rigid questionnaire to use in the interviews; we had instead a set of concerns that we wanted to explore, and the actual questions were determined more by the particular shape of each interview. In the sessions with individuals, we would usually begin by asking people how they saw their lives as different from their parents'. They usually responded by describing, in historical order, the significant events or experiences of their lives. Since so many of these concerned issues of powerlessness and adequacy, our problems in interviewing were not those of finding a context, but of understanding why these themes recurred again and again.

The staff for this project consisted of people with backgrounds similar to our own. Initially, a few of the people interviewed were asked if they would like to work as interviewers in turn, but most said they thought it would make them uncomfortable, because they would feel they were sitting in judgment. When we would then ask if they thought *we* were sitting in judgment, that characteristic break would occur—they told us not to take it personally, they liked us.

Although we interviewed about as many women as men, this book reflects primarily the experience of men. Examples are drawn from interviews with women when they elucidate something common to the experience of both sexes, when they show something about family life, or provide another perspective on the men interviewed. We worked this way for two reasons: first, this book explores a social order that affects men in a different way than women, simply because of the cultural valuation placed on the traditional work of men; second, a woman working with us, Claire Siegelbaum, has edited a companion volume of interviews that presents at firsthand the experience of working-class women.

We must say something about the changes we have made from what people actually told us to what appears on the printed page. None of the names used are real, and such revealing personal information as exact occupation or details of a marriage has also been altered. Moreover, we have taken certain liberties beyond those necessary to protect anonymity: in various instances we have condensed remarks people made; when statements two people made on an issue were very similar, we have portrayed them as coming from one person. In a few instances we have put words in people's mouths, words they were struggling for, we felt, but couldn't find. Twice we have combined elements from several life histories into one. We hope that the people interviewed will forgive us for pushing the presentation of their lives so close to the boundaries of fiction. It is for clarity and art that we have done so, though we hope it guards their privacy all the more.

This raises a question for you, the reader: how believable is what you read? Art creates a different truth from the recitation and interpretation of facts. We need, therefore, to show you why some measure of artful freedom has been necessary to us—why, in other words, we could not make a strictly scientific study of people's feelings about class and human dignity.

Any opinion poll or attitude survey with claims to scientific precision has to satisfy four conditions before it is put out in the field. The researcher first of all has to define some criterion by which he can judge the people he will interview as "representative" of other people's feelings. Then, he must decide what kind of questions will be meaningful to a person as a representative of some larger group. Third, he must find some way of boiling down the responses he gets so that he can make comparisons between different groups of people. Finally, he has to find a means, by random selection or otherwise, to gain access to individuals who are in fact representative of the given group.

A poll thus requires the pollster to know in large part what he is doing and what he wants before he talks to anyone. The great value of this is that he can create evidence in this way, by taking an issue where the terms are known, and seeing to whom they apply. When he asks a group of white workers, "Do you approve or disapprove of the way the

President is handling the Vietnam war?" he is going to get concrete answers. If, however, he asks, "What do you feel the President should do about the Vietnam war?," without supplying alternative answers, he is taking some risk; he is going to learn more about the complexities of personal feeling, but the answers may be so varied that he won't be able to boil them down to three or four characteristic responses. If he asks, still more generally, "What kind of role should a President play in making war?," he might get great richness of feeling in response, but the more he follows these up with each person, the harder and harder it will be to codify the complexities as clear evidence.

This doesn't mean that poll-takers can't ask profound questions; it does mean they face difficult problems in dealing with the ambiguities, subtleties, and contradictions involved in answers made in the same spirit. In our investigations, however, it was just this kind of subtlety that we were after.

To talk to people about their experiences, moreover, involves a measure of person-to-person trust that does not come from getting people's names in a directory and calling them up. It is very difficult to ring doorbells randomly in a neighborhood and ask people if they would like to sit down for three hours and tell you the story of their lives. For our interviews, therefore, we moved from person to person through contacts we developed in working-class communities in Boston. In the beginning we met people through nursery schools and parents' groups which we visited, or through priests. Then, increasingly, the people we interviewed helped us find others they thought might be interested.

44

Such an approach, of course, risks aimless wandering. This we tried to avoid by modeling the overall shape of the interviews so that the people mirrored in rough proportion the occupational and ethnic backgrounds of the white manual-laboring population in the Boston area. We did this to determine whether the issues of freedom and dignity in a life like Frank Rissarro's reappear among a diversity of people—and we found that indeed they do. But in this book we cannot make the kinds of claims a pollster would aim for, i.e., that Irish workers feel more anxiety than Italians, or that service workers feel they have had an unfair deal more than factory workers do.

We have tried as far as we could to see through the eyes of the workers talking. Sometimes, however, we have also tried to explain experiences they had but which we felt they did not fully understand; sometimes we have judged whether people were being dishonest or unfair, sometimes we have talked about issues that never came up in the discussions in order to make sense of those that did.

This unavoidable intrusion of ourselves makes it all the harder to say what is "representative" of workers in general, representative in the demographic terms a pollster would use. (Indeed, he would be rightly skeptical that any group of 150 people could "represent" 35 to 40 million.) The only way we can generalize is to turn the matter around and ask what is representative or characteristic of American society in its impact on the people interviewed. It is not so much as a replication of other workers that their lives ought to bear a larger witness, but as focused points of human experience that can teach something about a more general problem of denial and frustration built into the social order.

We should say a word about the notes and references in this book. Since we are writing for the general reader rather than the specialist, we have noted places in the text where a general reader might want to continue on his own by reading something else. A more extensive list appears in "Related Writings of Interest" at the end of the book.

AN OVERVIEW

To get an overview of the human problems faced by an American laborer, we can do no better than take Ricca Kartides for a guide. He is an exceptional man: a first-generation immigrant from Greece to a Boston where there is no longer a Greek enclave to shield him. But, more than this, he is an educated man of the middle class who in coming to America has been trapped into manual labor. He is a good guide because he is a man of our class, and a sensitive individual, trying to make sense of what it means to be an American worker. His reactions, we have often thought, reflect what might be our own if suddenly we became laborers.

Ricca Kartides emigrated twelve years ago from a small city in Greece, a town in which everyone knew everyone else; the people were friendly though overbearing, he recalls, and life proceeded at a slow and traditional pace. More educated and affluent than most of the townsfolk, Kartides held a teacher's degree. He was disliked, however, by his in-laws and by certain important members of his community who controlled all well-paying jobs. Finding himself in daily fear of losing his teaching post, and with the added burden of supporting a wife, he decided at age twenty-four that he had to leave. Like many immigrants before him, he knew very little about conditions in the New World: he chose not so much to come here as to leave an intolerable state of affairs at home.

Kartides arrived in America with $12 in his pocket, no understanding of English, and no recognized skills. He went to work in a factory, temporarily he thought, while he learned English. However, he found himself stuck doing unskilled labor; having to work long hours to provide for himself and his family, he had neither the time, the money, nor the energy to return to school for the credentials that would get him into a white-collar job in America.

"If I am an unskilled man, where else can I go but to clean? You don't need a degree to clean." A naturally gregarious man, Kartides first began to understand his decline through the coldness with which people once his equals now treated him. In contrast to the old country, he feels, the culture of Americans permits no sense of reciprocal respect across class boundaries: "Look, in Greece when I saw the janitor of my building at night, we would stop and chat for a moment; here a tenant is doing me a favor by being polite." He finds in America an absence of rituals by which people might transcend class lines.

Ricca describes his situation as one of having many acquaintances but no close friends. The lack of friendship, he says, "doesn't bother me at all, since my really close friends are my family. I'm the kind of person who, if I feel I'm not wanted I'm not getting involved at all. Some people . . . they go ahead and they *try*. With me, I have my own life, my own problems . . . so now why am I going to get involved in another one?"

When Kartides first began work as a maintenance man, he lived in an apartment where he received strict instructions to use the back door, and never let his children play on the empty lawn surrounding the building. He reacted to this impersonality by making heroic efforts of time, work, and personal sacrifice so that he could own a home of his own. His hope was that by freeing himself from other people's interferences, he could feel more confident about himself. It was not to own, not for economic gain, that he worked so hard for a private house; it was to gain a sanctuary, a living space where, in being only with his immediate family, he would not find his place in society thrown in his face over the smallest matters. The home is therefore for him the center of freedom, "and what I mean by freedom is my children can play without nobody telling them what to do."

Yet this search for sanctuary has left Kartides in a difficult position. He has bought property in a nearby suburb of Boston in order to be free, yet must work fourteen hours a day at two jobs in order to pay for his "freedom," leaving him scant time to enjoy his home. He bought property in order to create an independent sphere of living for himself and his family, yet, in the very process, finds himself sacrificing his social life to pay for this privilege. He makes repairs on his house, a modest one, to make it decent; yet since he is taxed for his improvements, he must work even longer. Since his house, like many residences in or near American cities, lacks access to good public transportation, he must buy a car, and that, too, takes money. And more money, for a man who cleans or paints houses or sells shoes, comes only from longer hours spent on the job and away from home.

He understands the trap in which he is caught. He knows

that the actions he has taken are not yielding the promised rewards; yet to do nothing, to be just "Ricca the janitor" who uses the back door and yells at his kids when they set foot on the apartment house grass, is unbearable. "So it was not because I wanted to make too much money; it was because I wanted to buy things, things I like, to live decently . . ."

"It seems to me," the interviewer observes, "that you really regret leaving Greece . . . Let me ask you something —do you really think you have to be a rich man to go back? Couldn't you go to another town there?"

"Well, you see . . . now I am what I am, a family man, a daddy, and . . . I feel I have a duty to them . . . a duty to make something of myself here in America where the children are born . . . so that they can respect me, you see . . . now I am a cleaner . . . now there is nothing wrong with that, that is my lot . . . so what I have to do is to make something of it."

One senses, however, that Ricca has given up on himself. He feels his life to be pretty much over (he is now thirty-six); the station he occupies he believes he will remain in the rest of his days. Even so, he is not resigned, for there seems one path of hope left: his children. It is they who can acquire dignity in anyone's eyes, if they increase their freedom by moving up to a higher class.

Kartides is proud, yet somewhat defensive, of the old-fashioned way in which he rears these children, teaching them manners, respect for their parents, and courtesy to others. He takes pride in not being a "permissive" parent, although he says he is more lax in his discipline than his parents ever were with him. "And all the children they come to

Daddy—because I'm the guy who brings the bread home. So they *have* to have some respect for me. I respect them because they are my children, but I am their daddy, so they have to . . . they have to follow the rules *I* set at home. And, and if I respect myself at home—me and my wife—my kids, they're going to see good examples. And they're going to learn how to behave in the way *I* behave."

His humiliation—that is a part of his strictness, but so also is a revulsion at the gulf between classes. His kids will treat all men with dignity: "If this is a world where you have a rat race, let it be. But at least *my* kids is going to be the way *I* want them." But don't those who refuse to join the rat race lose, aren't they beaten down by the more aggressive? This thought too has occurred to him, and there is a fear in Ricca that in making his kids humane he might also be condemning them to remain in his station.

It is difficult for Ricca Kartides, even as he creates some measure of material security in his life, to feel that his quantitative gains translate into the emotional sense of independence and assuredness he wants from these material improvements. He sees himself as receiving the ultimate form of contempt from those who stand above him in society: he is a function, "Ricca the janitor," he is a part of the woodwork, even though he makes $10,000 a year, owns a home, drives a car, and has some money in the bank for his children's education. He feels vulnerable and inadequately armed, but what has he done wrong?

These are the feelings working-class life in America arouses in an outsider.

PART ONE

THE SOURCES
OF INJURY

CHAPTER I

BADGES OF
ABILITY

When people talk about feeling inadequate or self-defeating, they often seem absorbed in themselves. They would never have such doubts, wrote the Renaissance philosopher Pico della Mirandola, if they did not live in the company of other men. In *An Oration on the Dignity of Man*, Pico argued that the concerns for what we call today personal legitimacy or adequacy stem from a search society inaugurates in all men for an image of the essential dignity of man. Animals live naturally from day to day without worrying about why they ought to live; men have that worry because of all the actions they take together, their love for and cruelty to one another, their enjoyment of living in more complicated ways than simple survival would demand.

What Pico wrote applies so well to the people we interviewed; Frank Rissarro, who has survived, indeed has triumphed over, material adversity, worries about his adequacy because he wants to love and be loved, because he has experienced so much cruelty, because he wants to be treated with respect—which is not the same thing as earning a fat paycheck.

The Hidden Injuries of Class

The search for human dignity seems like a positive action men undertake; history, however, shows that the images of human dignity in society can be enormously destructive.

Anthropologists speak of the "pseudo-speciation" practiced by certain tribes. The tribe's inner solidarity and cohesion have become so strong that the tribesmen believe their peculiar customs to form the standard by which all people ought to live; when the tribe comes across other groups who have different customs, why should it tolerate them, why should the tribe even care if it treats the outsiders with a brutality its members would never think of practicing among themselves? When belonging in a given society moves to the extreme of defining the dignity of all mankind, contempt and hostility towards those who differ celebrate the dignity of man.

Caste societies also create oppressive images of human dignity. The brahmin, the duke, the caliph have "worthiness" in the sense the monarchist Thomas Young used the term in 1615; the worthiness of mankind is visible only at its point of perfection in the highest caste; therefore, coercing those below is justified because the duke or caliph is morally superior to them, as well as more powerful.

But what of ourselves? Nations now sometimes act as self-righteous tribes, practicing genocide out of contempt; the strong still oppress the weak not only because they can, but because they feel entitled to do so. Against these actions there has come into being in the last two hundred years a set of ideas about the dignity of man that promises, at least, to make men feel such behavior is wrong.

The humanists of the eighteenth century preached an idea of the worthiness of all men, of a natural dignity in man regardless of his position in society or his power. These Enlightenment ideas of universal human dignity have become such clichés, it is now largely forgotten how radical they are. They seem to set Pico's dictum aside; for whether you are loving or cold, curious or self-contained, in advance of being a social animal you are by nature entitled to courtesy and decent treatment from anyone else. Deliverance from specialized, wounding images of humanity is what the Enlightenment promised, and that meant concretely deliverance from the exercise of wanton power by the state.

In America this Enlightenment image of humanity has been given a special cast. Our ideals have traditionally involved not just escape from the demands of the state, but from demands of the social bond itself. Throughout much of our history the loner, the self-reliant individual, the dropout, at odds with other men, appears as someone who can be respected and respect himself. The "Americanization" of Ricca Kartides, for example, is the transformation of a man who once sought respect as a member of a tight-knit community into one who has sought respect from others because he can take care of himself—in other words, because he can do without them. James, the municipal clerk's son who feels so lost in college, dreams of dropping out of school, getting himself together, finding some "decent way to pass the time," and then, perhaps, going back to the school community.

If you don't belong to society, society can't hurt you. A "pursuit of loneliness," Phillip Slater calls it, and yet it is a puzzle that it should exist in modern America at all. The greatest celebration of this pursuit occurred in a society that no one today would recognize as his own; the glorification of the lone man's dignity in such movements as transcendentalism rested on a set of assumptions that the janitor, the meat-cutter who made good, the prodigal son of the municipal clerk do not share.

While European celebrants of individualism like Adam Smith had argued that each man ought to be free to do as he liked in society, Emerson preached that the individual ought to replace society, to be so self-sufficient he could live as a world unto himself, foregoing the aid and even the companionship of other men. This paean to loneliness assumed that society would permit it. Emerson, Thoreau, and Whitman could speak of the transcendence of the self-sufficient individual because they believed society itself was weak. To them, the social bond made no profound calls on the human soul. Indeed, the evil in man was traceable to the weakness involved in living together, compromising, depending on one another. The transcendentalist view totally denies Pico's. It is not, however, a mirror for the thoughts of Kartides, Rissarro, or James: they do want community with others but feel they have to earn the right to communal respect by showing others they totally take care of themselves.

The society in which transcendentalism flowered made its ideas eminently plausible. In the America Tocqueville surveyed, men who were discontented with the communities into which they were born could simply leave and start anew by themselves. On the eve of the Civil War, most Americans were still independent farmers or small businessmen. To reject entangling alliances at home as well as abroad was indeed to make a virtue out of the facts of everyday life.

Corporate, metropolitan, technological America mirrors an opposite society. The small farmer and businessman languish in the face of large organizations. While in 1871 about seventy percent of the population was self-employed in these ways, now only five percent is.° This is a physically mobile society still, but the social landscape is acquiring such sameness that to move is no longer to leave behind. How is one to be a self-reliant loner in the land today?

That circumstances are now so different appeared to David Riesman twenty years ago to herald a new moral order, where sensitivity to others must replace aloneness and "inner direction": a man who follows his own fancy on the assembly line endangers others and holds up work; a researcher who does everything for himself does very little. The disorders in American society in recent years have seemed to wash away the last trace of moral plausibility from the ideas Emerson and Whitman held dear. Transcendentalists could speak of the trivial affairs of social man, and yet who would say that the racial, urban, and generational strife of the past few years has failed to have a profound impact on the individuals within society? To withdraw or shut out these conflicts from one's consciousness would seem, not the prelude to awakening virtue, but a passive acceptance of human injustice and arbitrary pain.

Given these realities, why then does independence matter so much to people like Frank Rissarro? When he thinks about his entry into the white-collar world, the "reward" of success for him is that he can act more independently, be

° T. B. Bottomore, *Classes in Modern Society* (New York: Random House; 1966); Victoria Bonnell and Michael Reich, *Workers and the American Economy* (Boston: New England Free Press; 1969).

more personally in control. Kartides, too, imagines dignity within the confines of manual labor to be the carving out of some social space in which he is alone. To be free for these people living in a corporate, interdependent society is to get on their own: why will such freedom give them dignity? If we can answer these questions, which are about hidden dimensions of individualism in a corporate society, we may be able to uncover the burden of class in that society: the feeling of not getting anywhere despite one's efforts, the feeling of vulnerability in contrasting oneself to others at a higher social level, the buried sense of inadequacy that one resents oneself for feeling.

ABILITY AS THE BADGE
OF AN INDIVIDUAL

In the last chapter, the contradictions of freedom and dignity in America were linked to a notion, vaguely sketched, of self-development through intellect and rational control. Furthermore, Rissarro, James, and Kartides believed that the higher a man's social position, the more chance he had to develop these internal powers. To know more about what self-development means, and the full bearing of social class on this psychological process, we now want to describe how certain psychological ideas about *ability* transform the concept of the *self* into the concept of the *individual;* that is, we want to try to clarify exactly how modern notions of ability have become entangled in the dilemma of freedom and dignity now confronting American society, a dilemma in which the individual—for all that corporate society should have made him out of date—continues to be a dream in men's minds of what kind of person now is free.

The pioneering psychologist E. L. Thorndike wondered in books like *Animal Intelligence* (1911) if ability could be expressed in terms of quantity and numbers. He saw that men exercised their intelligence in concrete actions and decisions, they manipulated objects in what were described as intelligent or unintelligent ways. Surely, if one could observe the physical effects of intelligence, one could make a physical measurement of the phenomenon itself. Then one could know "how much" intelligence was needed in the handling of a given situation, or "how much" intelligence a human being possessed.

Other researchers, like Binet and Simon, playing with this idea in such tests as the Stanford-Binet intelligence quotient exams, arrived at what seemed an important fact about society. The scores of those taking the tests were found overall to form a bell-shaped curve, with most people scoring around the middle, and fewer and fewer people being found as one moved toward the extremes of high and low I.Q. The conclusions at first drawn from this bell-shaped curve seem in retrospect extraordinary: here, the testers asserted, was a representation of the fixed, "natural" allotment of ability; the people who stood out as individuals were "naturally" unlike the mass at the center, either because they were very stupid or very smart. This interpretation inaugurated an enormously important social debate.

If intelligence is distributed in society this way, then what is the meaning of the phrase "All men are created equal"? Surely it is hard to accord equal respect to creatures of unequal genetic endowment. The questions become more sinister because certain ethnic and racial groups don't do as well, as a whole, on these tests as the white majority; the difference in scores has held on Army intelligence tests, for instance, for several decades.

. Some researchers in the tradition of the old experimental school have argued that these tests show real genetic differences between, say, blacks and whites. Arthur Jensen, studying pairs of twins adopted by parents of differing socio-economic background, has performed experiments which, he claims, show that nature rather than nurture or cultural bias is what the tests manifest. Hans Eysenck in England argues the same conclusion from different experiments.

The work of these men is so flimsy on scientific grounds that critics tend to lose sight of the issues in the debate: is intelligence a quantity, a given commodity in human beings at all? Even if the tests are biased in favor of white, middle-class standards, is there a genetic nature to be measured at all? It is known that the scores of individuals may show a fairly wide range of deviation from testing to testing, and that whole groups of "short-changed" people can improve their scores as test conditions are varied. If intelligence can be expressed at all as a tangible commodity, it is evidently like money or stock certificates in other respects as well: it can somehow be increased or lost, earned or squandered.

A fundamental challenge to the idea of intelligence-as-commodity has been posed by psychologists like Jean Piaget and Bärbel Inhelder in Geneva. Intelligence, they say, is rather a process changing over time and place to provide a repertoire of symbols that human beings need to understand their own phases of growth. This view has met a large measure of resistance in this country, for it would rob the psychologist of a peculiar kind of certainty: if he can compute the intelligence of a person, he can know something indelible, something fundamental, about that person; in other words, a person who is being measured in a test can be classified by it. The system of classification that results causes a few people to stand out as belonging to special classes of high or low, while the great majority are relatively indistinguishable in the middle.

Why should psychologists want to have such knowledge? We might broaden the question, since measures of ability by test and comparison have spread from the school to the office and factory: why is society so curious to know what abilities people have in this comparative and large-scale way? After all, the results can be perverted to destroy a fragile dream, only a few hundred years old, of equality among men.

Ironically, the impulse to determine a person's ability is also the child of the Enlightenment. In eighteenth-century France and England, bright sons of lower-bourgeois families demanded that government and professional positions be opened to persons on the basis of natural ability, rather than of parental influence or hereditary right. The minor lawyers of Paris in the 1780's are most identified with the cry of careers open to talent; but it appears as well in an essay of Voltaire's where he proclaims the common gift of reason spread among all humanity. For the lawyers and the philosopher there was a desire for liberation behind the cry, a desire to divorce men from the bonds of culture and past history. Such a celebration of natural talent leads logically to individualism: natural ability means the individual ought to be the master, rather than the prisoner, of culture.

The early intelligence-tester Alfred Binet once remarked, to the point, that measures of intelligence ought to give society a way to deal with the individual all by himself. Even Hans Eysenck, a believer in the genetic inequality of races, justifies the determination of talent as an enterprise that permits individuals of any race or group who have ability to be lifted out of the group context and treated on their own. The testing of ability acquires legitimacy in the eyes of its practitioners as the continuation of an old glorification of the individual apart from the social conditions into which he is born.

That ability is the badge of individual worth, that calculations of ability create an image of a few individuals standing out from the mass, that to be an individual by virtue of ability is to have the right to transcend one's social origins—these are the basic suppositions of a society that produces feelings of powerlessness and inadequacy in the lives of people like Rissarro, Kartides, and James. To connect ideology and the people, we need to understand what happens to people when they wear badges of ability. Two issues that emerge in recent studies of marital conflict are beginning clues to the personal effect of these values.

Whom shall I marry? That question seems obviously to be about *my* choice, about one of the most important controls I shall establish over my life. The more researchers probe that choice, however, the more they find a secret question, more destructive, more insistent, that is asked as well: am I the kind of person worth loving? This secret question is really about a person's dignity in the eyes of others; but it involves self-doubt of a peculiar kind.

An interchange from a study of "normal" marriages:

INTERVIEWER: Emile, you say you were saddled with a great anxiety when you first went out with Mary [his future wife]? . . .

EMILE: How did I know what she felt about me? . . . I mean, I felt sort of like I had to prove myself to her for her to love me, that whole *Playboy* thing . . . I guess in a way when I was trying to make an impression, it was less to impress her than impress me.

As William Goode has pointed out in his *World Revolution and Family Patterns*, questions like this seldom occur in societies where marriages are arranged; being chosen for marriage is out of the individual's control. When, however, the burden does fall on him or her, when it does become a matter of individual choice, the individual is faced with a terrible problem: if he or she is not chosen, then he or she may not be worth choosing. The more individual freedom, the more the essential worthiness of the individual becomes an issue in marriage.

When Emile talks about "proving himself," he is trying to cope with this threat to his self-worth; what Emile did to prove himself is typical of a pathetic and widespread phenomenon in our culture. He tried to validate his *self* to Mary by showing he had abilities and qualities that marked him off as an *individual* from the crowd—his taste in records, his opinions about politics, his skill at tennis. "I felt," said Mary, "he was so involved in showing how good he was, in proving himself, he wasn't really noticing *me*." In their early courtship, Emile nearly destroyed the relationship in this way. Only after Mary got it through to him that she cared for him, not whether he was good or bad at something, did their

63

relationship begin to deepen, and his various modes of validating the self drop away.

Wearing badges of ability, then, proves destructive to love in its early phases—perhaps because love cannot be earned or deserved: validated selves are objects rather than people. Yet there is another kind of family situation in which wearing a badge of ability makes, at least at first glance, more sense.

When strains in families develop as individuals grow apart in tastes, convictions, or interests, an inner conflict is often observed within the warring individuals about whether each one is "legitimate" enough to express the differences. In conflict between generations this search for legitimacy is clearest: the young feel entitled to break away when they can do something the parents can't, whether taking risks with drugs, adopting a different kind of politics, or acquiring a skill like playing the guitar the parents are too old to have. Ability is here more than a matter of taking tests. The children are legitimately interested in these new activities, to be sure; but in many families undergoing generational conflict, as Thomas Cottle points out, the actions the parents can't perform also serve to legitimate the child as someone with rights. The badge of ability, in other words, bestows the right to stand out as an individual.

It is with the converse of this proposition that serious trouble begins: if in order to be free you have to show you are different, what happens to the child who has nothing of his own to set against the parents? How does he or she legitimate the desire to be free? Out of this dilemma comes the sad anxiety one sees in so many adolescents, that search for styles of behavior they feel no real attachment to, no real pleasure in, but which are supposed to identify them as people who stand out. The "putdowns" adolescents practice on each other have this same motivation: if a kid can make a witty crack about someone else that makes the other feel inept or bumbling, he stands out, it is he who gets the attention, putting down the other.

Adults play the same game on many grounds, from competition about who has better things to competition about who is more radical. Hoping to stand out as individuals, people usually get involved in such games of aggressive inequality not for the pleasure of wounding others, but in order to validate themselves as distinctive, as having respect-able capacities.

Studies of career choice among college students show that decisions about what I want to do in life get entangled in this scheme of what I do well. A characteristic comment from one study: "I want to do physics, but I was much better graded in business practice, which is a drag of course, but I majored in that. . . ." Of course there is a pleasure in doing well what one likes to do; but people become afraid of doing things they think they would enjoy for fear they would be inept or no good—no good, that is to say, nothing special, not really any better than others. In this society, a scale of inequality can intrude on deciding what one desires, because the consciousness of human worth is a consciousness of self as individual, standing out from a mass who seem pretty much the same.

It might be said that this situation is hardly unique to our own times—the artists and craftsmen working in Italian cities at the time Pico wrote competed fiercely for personal honors by virtue of their ability to make furniture, intricate capes, or paintings. There is a difference, though. "I live on," Raphael once said, "in the strokes of paint"; the end was to create excellent things or to perform well. Modern notions of ability convert playing the guitar well or painting a picture into a *means*. Emile did not want to be good at things in order to be good at them; he wanted to use his prowess as a means of earning Mary's love. And yet it was not even true that he wanted to be loved for how good he was—the relationship in fact deepened only when he was loved for himself, not for his ability. Badges of ability are only useful as magnets to attract others.

To talk about an individual now recognized by badges of ability is to talk about a constructive force and a destructive one. The constructive force is the dream that these badges will fulfill an age-old demand for the dissolution of social position by inheritance or family connections. The self-destructive force is the self-defeating effect of these badges of ability as means of earning respect. In the family, they bring estrangement in courtship, hostility on one side and an aimless self-inflation on the other during periods of generational strife. In friendships, badges of ability often take the degenerate form of aggressive comparisons and putdowns. Badges of ability, finally, corrode an individual's sense of what he wants to do, as opposed to what will earn him respect from others. All these are perhaps manifestations of one truth: love in truth can never be earned or deserved.

But the family tensions illustrate a second kind of destructiveness. The man in love, the child rebelling put an enormous weight on how well they can perform; if the performance doesn't earn respect, then who is at fault? To be an individual has historic connotations of self-reliance, confidence, self-affirmation. The kind of individualism that appears in these family scenes, necessarily failing its end, threatens the person involved with a feeling of inadequacy, a feeling he is unloved because he hasn't proved himself to be good enough; therefore he tries still harder. Emile and Mary were lucky she was strong enough to remove them both from this bind. So much of the loneliness in our culture, however, comes from the vicious circle people get caught up in when they try to prove they are adequate enough to be loved.

Finally, these family scenes show how ability as the badge of a worthy self creates unequal classes of actors. The early I.Q. testers believed in a bell-shaped curve of ability, with fewer and fewer people having more and more ability. Let us not worry about the scientific shakiness of this idea. The image is important because on the most intimately personal level it appears to people as a way to decide who can wear the badge. In these struggles for worth there are two classes, the many and the few; the selves of the many are in limbo, the selves of the few who have performed win respect. But the few need the many: individuals exist only so long as a mass exists, a point of reference consisting of others who seem pretty much alike.

We have concentrated on the declarations of self that seek to put a person in the class of the few. What of the many? There is nothing wrong with being average, E. L. Thorndike once said. The remark is instructive. Those engaged in testing do not often speak of the mass as stupid, untalented, or empty, nor does a personnel supervisor speak of the perfectly competent but not outstanding employees in such harsh terms. Average, adequate, ordinary: it is a language wherein personal recognition of the few is balanced by impersonal toleration of the many; it is a matter of good versus neutral. Indeed, if harsher terms were used, if there were a strong sense that it was wrong for people to be average, then the people to whom these terms were applied would for just that reason become noticeable. The creation of badges of ability requires the mass to be invisible men.

Mass and masses—here we come a step closer to seeing what hidden dimensions of class underlie badges of individual ability. The search for dignity at the intimate level of family or friends requires an image of social inequality; social inequality in our society has as its base a mass of people who work with their hands. Is the sense of powerlessness among the workingpeople we interviewed related to this search for respect through signs of unequal ability? Are workers' feelings of inadequacy in the midst of materially coping with life related to the inadequacy this scheme of values creates?

To take another step, we need to expand the connection between the many, in the scheme of individualism we have initially sketched here, and the term "masses," with its historic connections of worker, proletariat, laborer.

One of the most revealing episodes in the recent history of American public opinion was the creation of the "hard hat," a racist, nationalistic soul opposed to any social change, who only wants more attention paid to his own problems. The ingredients of the stereotype were discredited by some careful research almost as soon as the image took form; manual laborers were no more in favor of making war than the rest of the nation—indeed, this research indicated that as a group they became more rapidly disen-

chanted with the current American war than suburban businessmen.°

Now, why should this image have so easily taken hold
among conservatives or righteous liberals or, for a while,
among workers themselves, as a picture of what they were
supposed to be? That image takes social ideals and subjects
them to a hidden agenda: the "right things" to think are believed by a few, by a vocal minority, and these people stand
socially higher than the silent majority. They think themselves "better" because they believe in what they consider
universal values—peace, brotherhood, freedom, and so on.
On that hidden agenda, the educated upper-middle-class
people who uphold the "right" values stand out from a mass
whose understanding and sensitivity they believe inferior to
their own; the hard hats, or the workers in the film Z, don't
have the brains to realize they are being manipulated by
those forces in power.

What of the mass in this scheme, what is the reaction of
the hard hat himself? The image becomes for him grounds
for denouncing the people who attempt to put him to shame
in this way, denouncing them for setting themselves up as
better than he. Indeed, if they really were so humane, their
professions of belief shouldn't make him feel inadequate or
ashamed. The hidden agenda behind this stereotype involves, then, genuine feeling the moment the question of a
"putdown" arises. The question of genuine feeling in fact

° Again, white laborers' racial attitudes are subject to many of the same complex
pressures that affluent professionals and businessmen are moved by: distance from
black settlements, work with blacks on the job, and so on, being more important in
forming "tolerant" behavior than simple measures of job position or even education, under some circumstances. The best recent work in these areas is by Hal
Shepperd, at the Upjohn Institute.

concerns both sides, for if studies of attitudes about war and race are accurate, the worker and the suburban professional have been all along pretty close in their specific views.*

Hidden agendas like this connect working-class masses to "mass" in the scheme of individual, distinctive ability. Inability to live up to a standard, in this case a failure to understand a standard of social justice, appears as a mass phenomenon, with the standard being determined by, and demonstrated in, the behavior of an elite minority. Nationalism and racism are not unknown among manual laborers, obviously; but when these things are spoken of as *their* problem, as attitudes characteristic of them as opposed to other Americans, the invitation becomes strong to set up a kind of moral individualism in which the educated few will stand out. It is at this point that an undeclared war over questions of dignity and genuine feeling breaks out.

An explicit consignment of manual laborers to the limbo of nonability has been made by sociologists like S. M. Lipset in theories about "working-class authoritarianism." Lipset argues that the limited experience, the narrow routine, and paltry cultural resources available to the manual laborer have the effect of limiting his ability to comprehend "rational" systems of political right and democratic behavior. The essence of the professor's argument is that the narrowness of working-class experience makes the worker too simple-minded to deal with the complexities of democratic morality or of pluralistic politics.

---

* Andrew Greeley has observed, quite fairly, that positive beliefs in social change are held by workers and suburbanites for entirely different reasons; why this might be so, in terms of a hidden dimension of class, we shall take up in the next chapter.

There is, to be sure, a seeming humanity in this argument: Lipset is saying that workers are not innately stupid, rather that their social circumstances have numbed their minds; faced with pluralistic strife or contending ideologies, they seek some authoritarian leader to reinstate law and order.

The professor is rather numbed by complexity himself. In *Political Man*, where these views are set forth in a chapter explaining the affinity of workers for communism, the succeeding chapter explains why fascism is mainly a middle-class phenomenon. Is fascism therefore not authoritarian, or is each class, like Tolstoy's unhappy families, authoritarian in its own way, or . . . ? But the assumptions behind this argument are more important than its weaknesses even in its own terms. For here is an old socialist arguing that man is no more than the creature of his circumstances, and that the circumstances of working-class life prevent people from developing the social intelligence necessary to deal with democratic strife.

The images of hard-hat or working-class authoritarianism are not really new. They are a new reading of a morality of social class that, in America, extends back to the first great industrial expansion in the decades following the Civil War.

The Horatio Alger stories describe a boy who moves out of the horrors of poverty into the middle classes because the boy possesses personal intelligence, has a sense of honor and fair play, and, incidentally, a fair share of luck. A fall in social standing appears in some European novels of the time, like *Vanity Fair*, as a matter of bad luck; in the United States, however, as one of the authors pointed out in a previous book, *Families Against the City*, a move downward more often had moral overtones: the clerk or accountant who became a factory worker failed because he lacked the ability to survive, his low social position was a reflection of the feebleness of his talents.

When socialist critics in this country and England attacked the new capitalistic order as oppressive, its defenders put up a peculiar rebuttal. Drawing on a bastardized version of Darwinian evolution, they made no claims that poverty was a passing phenomenon; they said, rather, that the fittest would survive it by escape into a higher class. Industrial society is hard, hard as animals in nature find the struggle to survive—a life-and-death battle. The justice of industrial capitalism in America, said Andrew Carnegie, is that society *here* will not fail to reward a man of talent. If a man is worthy of escaping poverty's terrors, he can do so.

If he doesn't have the ability to "make it," by what right does he complain?

This brand of individualism is certainly different from the doctrine preached by Emerson and Thoreau. They expounded an escape from the social bond itself, rather than escape from one class to another. The new doctrine seems on the surface much too fierce to belong in the same class as the repugnance towards hard hats voiced by war protesters or the misgivings voiced by analysts of working-class authoritarianism; these latter, after all, are critics of the world Andrew Carnegie once defended. But past contains the present in germ; once again, a few stand out, they escape the degradation of the masses, they have more in them as individuals that can be respected.

It is this conception of the individual that has affected

both William Pfaff and Jean Paul Sartre in their attitudes towards workers. For Pfaff, and for many upper-class radicals, the divide between the individual and the mass in terms of ability, in terms of very personal characteristics, makes it plausible that only an elite can now be a revolutionary force in America. For Sartre, the anxiety over his own capacity to write two thousand pages on Flaubert comes from a fear—is it of himself, is it of what others will think?—that such work is justified because, while the propaganda tract serves the needs of the masses, the writer or man of culture is so much more complex and individually developed that he *deserves* thousands of pages of analysis.

Carl Dorian, the electrician, James, the college student, Frank Rissarro, the meat-cutter turned bank clerk, are all touched by this conception of the individual as well. Looking up the ladder of social hierarchy from where they stand, they imagine they see fewer and fewer people who have been allowed the freedom to develop personal resources that others will value. They are ambivalent about this image, like Sartre—but in a somewhat different way. They resent the fact that society has created a split between the many, who are just ordinary workers, and the few individuals who are members of the professional and upper-middle classes; yet despite this resentment, when they think of themselves personally as lost among the many, they are also afraid that there may be some truth to this image.

Historians know very little about how poor people in cities reacted to the ideologies of class that took form five generations ago. In a way, it would at the time have been nonsensical for a steel worker or garment worker to get emotionally involved in how or whether his abilities had placed him in a certain position in society. At hand were much more terrible material penalties for being a worker: he went hungry, and so did his children; when illness or some other family crisis struck and he could not work, he was a doomed man.

While the lot of many white American manual laborers today remains precarious, the sheer physical degradation of the sweatshops or mills is gone for most. Indeed, in terms of income, amount of taxing physical exertion, and styles of living, the lines are not now sharp between many blue-collar and low-level office workers. To conclude that class differences are therefore disappearing would be wrong, however. What episodes like the hard-hat debate and the writings on authoritarianism suggest is that the lines of class difference are being redrawn.

Freedom is no longer simply the freedom to eat. Now it is a matter of how much choice a person has, and the development of human resources of men and women in a post-scarcity society. Classes of human beings can still be usefully defined by their productive function—but, as shall presently appear, class distinctions in both productive and emotional terms are growing sharper than they were under the old conditions of scarcity. "Mass," in the sense that the word applies to men like Rissarro or Kartides, refers to the kind of work where people do not feel they express enough that is unique in themselves to win others' respect as individuals; "elite," in the sense Pfaff or Sartre may use the term, refers to people who have become so complex they must be treated as special cases. Overlying these distinctions is a morality of shaming and self-doubt.

It is an accursed freedom that is at issue here. The terms

of individual freedom are so defined that in demonstrating special merit, a man or woman is no closer to validating the dignity of the self. And yet, when we introduce social class into the matter, the focus on the mass in this scheme, the issue is one of alienation *a priori*, a constriction felt by workers in their freedom of choice and of self-development.

In his critical study of Marx's economics, Louis Althusser makes some remarks that can also help orient a social-psychological approach to class.° There is too much of a tendency, Althusser says, to regard different classes of people as living in different worlds. One speaks of the alienation of labor, for instance, thinking of workers bored by the tedium of the machine, but seldom of the manager bored by pushing papers. Of course these experiences feel entirely different to the persons involved, but they have the same root cause. To have class differences, you must have a "generator," a common force or structure that divides people up.

The position we take in this book is that everyone in this society, rich and poor, plumber and professor, is subject to a scheme of values that tells him he must validate the self in order to win others' respect and his own. When the plumber makes this attempt, however, the feelings involved are quite different than when a professor does it. The examples we have so far given of assertion of individual ability in families point to three general results of such assertion: the search for respect is thwarted; the individual feels personally responsible for the failure; the whole attempt accustoms him to think that to have individual respect you must have social inequality. The plumber has a radically different experience of these phenomena than the professor because of where he

° Louis Althusser *et al.*, *Reading Capital* (London: New Left Books; 1970).

stands in the society and what he does. The association of mass with masses suggests that he will have a harder time asserting himself at all because other people—people higher up and even, perhaps, people like himself—think he doesn't have as much ability to start with as does a professor. But, if the matter is this simple, then all that's involved is a matter of class prejudice: just change people's minds to believe everyone has *some* special ability, and everyone can suffer in the same way.

The matter isn't that simple. The reason the "prejudiced" image exists at all is that it serves a purpose, as does this whole scheme of individuals recognized and respected by virtue of ability. This purpose is to continue the iniquities of the world of nineteenth-century industrial capitalism—on new terrain. And just as the material penalties of the old capitalism fell hardest on the workers, despite the fact that both rich and poor might be alienated by the work, so now the moral burdens and the emotional hardships of class are the thorniest and most concentrated among manual laborers. What we hope to do, then, is to illumine a hidden scheme of values that sorts men into different classes; but we hope to demonstrate this burden of class by exploring its impact on those who lose the most by being classified.

AN AUTHORITY JUDGES
FREEDOM AND DIGNITY

Class, in the sense writers like Marx, Saint-Simon, and Proudhon used the term in the nineteenth century, was a matter of power. Different classes of men existed in society because some men had control of other men's labor, and most men were not masters of what they did or made. In his *Sociological Tradition*, Robert Nisbet observes that at the end of the last century, a change occurred in the concept of the relationship between class and power: writers like Max Weber added a new dimension, embodied in the concept of "authority." A worker can know his foreman has power over him, and yet if only a matter of brute coercion is involved, why doesn't the worker rise up against the foreman when the latter takes unfair advantage of him? Why is it so hard for the oppressed to revolt against injustice? To answer such questions, men like Weber and Gramsci sought to describe the transformation of power into legitimate rule. They asked what values society spawns to legitimize the right of some to control the lives of many, convincing the worker that he *ought* to submit his labor to the will of others.

This idea of legitimacy is rather more complex than it first appears. If a man feels he obeys someone he ought to obey, what happens to his own self-image? The foreman tells a worker he will have to work extra hours if he wants to keep his job during depression times; the worker's freedom is thus diminished, of course, but if the worker feels the foreman has the right to take away his freedom, how can the man feel he has *any* rights, how can he respect himself? The rule might follow, tentatively, that when power becomes legitimate, whatever dignity a man accords to his ruler he must necessarily deny himself.

Now a badge of ability seems the perfect tool to legitimatize power. This concept of human potential says that the few are more richly endowed than the many and that only the few can know themselves—i.e., recognize themselves as distinctive individuals. Having gained "more" dignity by virtue of greater personal power, it is logical that they ought to rule the many. Apply to that simple meritocratic argument the tentative rule proposed above about legitimized power: the more inclined are the many, the masses, to a belief that dignity exists in these terms, and the more they surrender their own freedom to the few, the less chance they have of respecting themselves as people with any countervailing rights.

If, however, the people we encountered in the course of writing this book taught us anything, it is that this set of notions is all wrong, because the people who are subject to limits on their freedom do not take the dignity away from themselves that they accord to higher classes—as though dignity were a commodity. They react to power in a much more complicated way: look at Frank Rissarro's attitude toward "educated" work, for example. Educated men can control themselves and stand out from the mass of people ruled by passions at the bottom of society; that badge of ability earns the educated dignity in Rissarro's eyes. Yet the content of their power—their ability considered in essence rather than in relation to his personal background and memories—this he finds a sham, and repugnant. Still, the power of the educated to judge him, and more generally, to rule, he does not dispute. He accepts as legitimate what he believes is undignified in itself, and in accepting the power of educated people *he* feels more inadequate, vulnerable, and undignified.

The feelings he, and the other men and women we encountered, have about power in relation to their own freedom and dignity, demand some kind of fresh explanation. All these people feel society has limited their freedom more than it has limited that of middle-class people—by which they mean society has limited their freedom to develop powers inside themselves, not just restricted how much money they can make—but they are not rebellious in the ordinary sense of the word; they are both angry and ambivalent about their right to be angry.

For ourselves, a start in making sense of this complexity came in thinking back on observations one of us, Richard Sennett, had made sometime before in a school—not in the Boston area—of how teachers and students dealt with badges of ability. For, as he realized in retrospect, in that childhood setting there occurred intersections of power and authority, on the one hand, with freedom and dignity, on the other, that closely paralleled the experience of the adults we encountered in the present study.

Josiah Watson Grammar School° is an old red-brick building with a simple but well-kept playground. It is a large school, in the midst of an urban neighborhood of mostly three-decker houses. In the community surrounding the school live groups of Irish, Italian, and old-stock New Englanders, but almost all are manual laborers. The median family income in the neighborhood is about $8000—neither poor nor affluent.

The rooms at the Watson School evoke the interiors of the children's homes: old, rather run down, and yet clean, almost austere. In each schoolroom the only decorations

---

° A fictitious name, like those of the individuals in this book.

consist of an American flag, a bound set of maps, and a plaque with the Pledge of Allegiance. The school desks are new—tubular steel legs holding up flat wooden boxes. In them, children's supplies are neatly arranged, even for the littlest children. The teachers take a certain pride in this, but they apologize to the visitor for the tops scratched with the obscene words, drawings, and initials that children always seem to inflict on such objects.

The classes in Watson School, even as low as the second grade, jolt the outsider who has lost touch with the institutional life of children. Everything that goes on in the second-grade class, from reading preparedness to play with toys, is directed by the teacher. She takes great pains to see that the children act "good and proper." The visitor who is aware of his own presence in these classrooms at first thinks this show of discipline, this constant commanding and watching, is the teacher's response to that presence. After the teacher relaxes and forgets he is there, however, the discipline continues. It varies among the teachers from harsh to loving; but all those in charge of classrooms at the Watson School act like conductors who must bring potentially unruly mobs of musicians under their direction. As the principal remarks, "It is by establishing authority that we make this school work."

In Watson School, teachers restrict the freedom of the children because these figures of authority have a peculiar fear of the children. It is the mass who seem to the teachers to threaten classroom order, by naughty or unruly behavior; only a few are seen as having "good habits" or the right attitude. As one teacher explained, "These children come from simple laborers' homes where the parents don't understand the value of education." Yet in the early grades the observer noticed few examples of disruptive behavior. He sensed among the six- and seven-year-olds a real desire to please, to accept the teacher's control and be accepted by her. One pathetic incident, although extreme, stands out. In the middle of a reading-preparedness class, a child wet his pants because he was absorbed in his lesson. "What can you do with children like that?," the teacher later remarked in a tone of disgust.

What happens is that the teachers act on their expectations of the children in such a way as to *make* the expectations become reality. Here is how the process worked in one second-grade class at Watson School—unusual in that it was taught by a young man. In this class there were two children, Fred and Vincent, whose appearance was somewhat different from that of the others: their clothes were no fancier than the other children's, but they were pressed and seemed better kept; in a class of mostly dark Italian children, these were the fairest-skinned. From the outset the teacher singled out these two children, implying that they most closely approached his own standards for classroom performance. To them he spoke with a special warmth in his voice. He never praised them openly by comparison to the other children, but a message that they were different, were better, was spontaneously conveyed. As the observer watched the children play and work over the course of the school year, he noticed these two boys becoming more serious, more solemn, as the months passed. Obedient and never unruly from the first, by the end of the year they were left alone by the other children.

By then they were also doing the best work in the class.

The other children had picked up the teacher's hidden cues that their performance would not be greeted with as much enthusiasm as the work of these two little boys. "It's not true of the other children that they generally have less potential," the teacher remarked. "It's a question of not developing their ability like Fred and Vincent. I know you're right, I tend to encourage them more despite myself, but I—it's obvious to me these little boys are going to make something of themselves."

In the Watson School, by the time the children are ten or eleven the split between the many and the few who are expected to "make something of themselves" is out in the open; the aloofness developing in the second grade has become open hostility by the sixth. Among the boys, this hostility is expressed by images which fuse sex and status. Boys like Fred and Vincent are described by the "ordinary" students as effeminate and weak, as "suck-ups." The kids mean by this both that the Freds and Vincents are getting somewhere in school because they are so docile, and that only a homosexual would be so weak; the image of a "suck-up" crystallizes this self-demeaning, effeminate behavior that to them marks off a student whom the institution can respect.

What has happened, then, is that these children have directed their anger at their schoolmates who are rewarded as individuals rather than at the institution which is withholding recognition of them. Indeed, the majority of boys in the fifth and sixth grades are often not consciously in conflict with the school at all. Something more complex is happening to them.

These "ordinary" boys in class act as though they were serving time, as though schoolwork and classes had become something to wait out, a blank space in their lives they hope to survive and then leave. Their feeling, apparently, is that when they get out, get a job and some money, *then* they will be able to begin living. It is not so much that they are bored in school—many in Watson School like their classes. It is rather that they have lost any expectation that school will help them, that this experience will change them or help them grow as human beings.

One teacher in this school, an enthusiastic young woman who liked to work with "ordinary" students, said her greatest problem was convincing the students that they could trust her. The other teachers and the principal disapprove of her because she runs her class in an informal manner. They feel she lets the students "get away with anything," "that she can't keep discipline." Permissiveness is a vice, order a necessity, in the minds of the other teachers; they believe that most of their charges, due to family class background and past school performance, will resist following the rules which to an educated adult seem so logical and beneficial. It is not that these teachers are intentionally mean, but that they unwittingly set in motion in the classroom a vicious circle that produces exactly the kind of behavior they expect.

There is a counterculture of dignity that springs up among these ordinary working-class boys, a culture that seeks in male solidarity what cannot be found in the suspended time that comprises classroom experience. This solidarity also sets them off from the "suck-ups." Hanging around together, the boys share their incipient sexual exploits, real and imagined; sex becomes a way to compete within the group. What most cements them as a group, however, is the breaking of rules—smoking, drinking, or taking drugs together, cutting classes. Breaking the rules is an act "nobodies" can share with each other. This counter-culture does not come to grips with the labels their teachers have imposed on these kids; it is rather an attempt to create among themselves badges of dignity that those in authority can't destroy.

A full circle: outside observers—parents, teachers, and others—who see only the external aspects of this counter-culture, are confirmed in their view that "hanging around" is destructive to a child's self-development. Dignity in these terms exacts a toll by the standards of the outer world.

The division of children, in schools like Watson, into groups with a shared sense of loyalty and individuals alone but "getting somewhere," characterizes many levels of education; it is not something unique to, say, college-bound youth as opposed to vocational school boys. Studies of trade schools show the same phenomenon occurring: boys who are good at car mechanics in school start to feel cut off from others, even though the possession of those skills might make them admired by their less-skilled peers outside of school. It is an institutional process that makes the difference, a question of mere toleration versus active approval from those in power.

The drama played out in the Watson School has as its script the assigning and the wearing of badges of ability like those described earlier, worn by adults. The teachers cast the Freds and Vincents into the role of Andrew Carnegie's virtuous man. Ability will make these children into individuals, and as individuals they will rise in social class. The mass find themselves in a role similar to that which Lipset assigns to adult workers: their class background allegedly limits their self-development, and the counterculture of compensatory respect they create reinforces, in a vicious circle, the judgments of the teachers.

The teacher has the *power* to limit the freedom of development of his or her students through this drama. But why is he or she moved to act in this repressive way? This question is really two questions: it is first a matter of a teacher legitimizing in his own mind the power he holds, and second, a matter of the students taking that power as legitimate.

The teachers are in a terrible existential dilemma. It is true that they are "prejudiced" against most of their students; it is also true that they, like all human beings, want to believe in the dignity of their own work, no matter how difficult the circumstances in which they have to work seem to them. If a teacher believed that every single student would perpetually resist him, he would have no reason to go on teaching—his power in the classroom would be empty. A teacher needs at least a responsive few in order to feel he has a *reason* to possess power. The few will confirm to him that his power to affect other people is real, that he can truly do good. To sort out two classses of ability, then, in fear of the "lower" class of students, is to create a meaningful image of himself as an authority rather than simply a boss.

It is true that an analysis at this level of teachers, or other power figures dealing with working-class people, is by itself inadequate. A teacher may be having an existential crisis, but that doesn't explain why images of social class and classes of ability have come to fuse in his mind, nor does it explain how useful, how convenient, this crisis of self-legitimacy is in keeping the present class structure going. Still, it is important to keep before ourselves the experiential reality facing a person who has power over others. The teachers at Watson did not think of themselves as tools of capitalism, or even as repressive. They felt they had to legitimize their own work's dignity in the face of working-class students; and making a moral hierarchy on the basis of ability—however artificially and unjustifiably—was the natural means they used.

The perceptions the children had of the teachers similarly concerned not their power, but their legitimacy.

The observer is playing marbles with Vinny, a third-grader, described by his teacher as an "unexceptional, average student who tolerates school," and Vinny begins absent-mindedly to arrange the marbles in sets by color. The observer points out to him that he is doing something like what the teacher had asked him to do in arithmetic hour and he hadn't then been able to do. Vinny replies, "I didn't want to give her no trouble"—an answer the observer notes without, at the time, understanding what Vinny meant. In a class on grammar, Stephanie gives a past participle incorrectly; the teacher asks her to try again, but while she is thinking, one of the bright children interrupts with the right answer. The teacher—the experimental and "permissive" woman already described—tells the bright child to shut up and gives Stephanie another example to work out. Stephanie looks at her in total surprise, wondering why the teacher should still care about whether *she* can learn to do it, if the right answer has already been provided. Max, an obnoxious fifth-grade bully, has somehow formed an interest in writing dog-gerel rhymes. During a composition hour he reads one, but when he finishes, the teacher makes no reply, merely smiles and calls on the next pupil. Asked later how he felt, Max looks a little crestfallen and says with characteristic grace, "Lookit, shithead, she ain't got time to waste on me."

The child can read only the culmination of the teacher's feelings, the teacher's behavior in making a moral separa-tion of the many and the few by ability; he cannot read the teacher's mind. An adult observer would have to spend hours with that second-grade teacher at Watson School, after all, to get the man himself to understand what he was doing. All the child can know is that morally tinged judg-ments are being made about his ability to perform, and that he must use his ability in a manner that wins the teacher's respect.

Authority for the teacher is a matter of personal assertion, assertion of his power to do good as opposed to his mere possession of power. Authority appears to the child, how-ever, as *passive*, as an audience before whom he must prove himself. The very tolerance of the teacher, the apposition of good to neutral, makes this so. The child feels he is on trial, that he is responsible, like Vinny or Max, for using his abil-ity; the teacher is a judge to him, not a prosecutor. It is not so much when the many are openly scolded that they feel the most pressure from the teacher—at such a time he is showing some real concern about them. It is when the kids are trying to be good that the teacher's power is most felt. At that time, the message they get is that something is wrong with them in the eyes of this silent judge who does not, who cannot, verbalize his distance. It is up to them to cross the barrier by asserting themselves as individuals. But to act here is to be trapped in a painful dilemma.

The child can try to win respect from a figure in power, alienating his peers but confirming to the judge that here is an individual who is going to make something of himself in life, i.e., move up socially. The child can try to win respect from his peers, but in that case he feels that he has not developed the abilities within himself that would earn him the respect of a powerful person in a higher class.

The situation seems clearly self-defeating. But why, then, don't those caught up in it rebel? It is true that the teacher is usually the first adult outside the family to give the children new experience. Indeed, the teachers at Watson School receive the accolades of the parents as a very important figure in the children's lives. In homes where the parents have limited education, the stress on the teacher's role is especially strong: the teacher can open the gateway to opportunities the parents never had.

The child's own experience in school, however, is most important. Since the teacher appears to him as passive, is it not his own fault if he fails to catch the teacher's attention? The system must work, for the child can see that a few are chosen—but not he. Could he have paid more attention, worked harder? He wants and needs friends; since he cannot read the teacher's mind, how can he know that forming friendships based on "hanging around," mutual defense, and breaking small rules, reinforces the teacher's belief that he hasn't much intellectual ability? Before the passive judge, some people make it, while the teacher tolerates *him* impersonally—that is what he knows. All the burden of the situation seems on him; indeed, since the teacher does tolerate him, there is nothing in this passive, judgmental authority that he feels he can fight.

To put this school situation in general terms, we may say that this is an instance of how a superior "gets away with" restricting the freedom of someone in his charge by replacing the problem of limited freedom with the problem of the inferior person asserting his own dignity—the superior will not control, he will impassively judge. This is a game of disguising power, but it is not a game in which the powerful consciously tries to "get away with" duping people in his charge or deceiving them. The game works because, in a school like this, *all the actors genuinely believe they are engaged in problems of self and in morally meaningful personal actions that transcend power;* in this drama of class and age, power becomes legitimate to those it wounds through the very means by which the powerful seek to convince themselves that, faced with inferior people, they can at least do some good.

Weber despaired of people ever breaking the bonds of legitimized power in a class society, except in very special cases. The situation in the Watson School shows an instance of how power is legitimized and maintained, not by rigidly tyrannical measures, but rather by a subtle and delicate balance. The children have a great deal of resentment against the aspersions on their dignity the teacher's power ultimately causes; but they don't know what to do about that anger, or even, because they see the teacher as passive, who is to blame. So they turn on the few who are approved, leveling at the Freds and Vincents all the accusations of weakness and inability to command respect that the authority figures implicitly level against *them*—though Max and Vinny do not blame the "suck-ups" for their own position in the classroom. The legitimization of power is like a cloak of secrecy over the origins of one's anxiety. It is this cloak of secrecy that makes these children feel responsible for a situation they did not create.

It is of course true that children do not have the developed awareness of adults, but the situation we have described in Watson School is an adult problem beamed at children. We want now to show how this problem is beamed at adults, how this school situation is a paradigm of the problems of freedom and dignity created by legitimized authority. Yet we hope to show how the greater self-awareness of working-class adults does not remove this cloak of secrecy over the origins of troubled dignity, but makes the problem all the more intense.

"I don't know if I'm coming across with a chip on my shoulder or something," says George Corona, "but I . . . there are a lot of people that I direct that I feel really just have no competence in what they're doing, but got the job . . . they're there, they do the menial labor, they call themselves electricians, they do the kind of things that I think kids out of grade school could do, but they call themselves electricians and they're making good salaries." George Corona is a senior foreman for an aerospace firm that does minor production for a missile project. He describes himself as a little above the "drones" and far below the scientist.

George Corona resembles the teachers in Watson School

in that he feels himself confronted by a mass without real talent. The teachers, however, can legitimize their power in this situation by finding a few individuals hidden in the mass who have real ability; George Corona, by contrast, needs to see that everyone produces. If only a few have talent in his eyes, his problems as a foreman are even worse. How can the other workers also be made effective enough to produce up to standard?

The fear of being powerless is reinforced by his view of his position in relation to his own superiors. "I've come to see I'm responsible *to* people, and what gets—I don't make the rules, so how can I be . . . I mean responsible?" He does not consider that his subordinates might harbor the same feelings in relation to him; he does not forgive them.

George Corona is not when alone a mean or disagreeable person. In talking alone with him, the interviewer began to sense that he was very much afraid of being "dragged down," of "falling into nothingness." These metaphors marked not only his description of family life for many of his friends, but his interpretation of what was happening more generally to the social fabric of the country. Yet the facts of George's own life suggest contrasting metaphors: his parents were both laborers, and he studied mechanical drafting at night while working as a short-order cook for several years; he has made a rather dramatic rise. It might seem that he sees in the men below him an image of his past, and that in feeling contempt for them, he displays anxiety about his own rise and the security of his position. Perhaps that is true (although these "drones" are infinitely better off than his parents ever were), but his situation at work makes him feel at once harsh and inadequate. The essential characteristic he sees in his subordinates is that they form a homogeneous mass, and he explains this by an absence of ability that would distinguish any of them. Such feelings are now familiar, but what about his feelings toward himself? In a large corporation, he stands out from them, but as he says, his superior position means his work consists of taking responsibility for their work to his own superiors—so that, if they are just drones, his placement in the corporate structure results in the terrible irony that he, who has in theory risen, is a prisoner of the mass, not a ruler of them, "and like I don't have any real independence." He would like to make the rules; this would give him real power, yet supervision is not power because he feels dependent on these men he does not respect. In the end, his disrespect for them has fused into a very strong sense of disrespect for his own work.

In the world of child and teacher, the dominant figure can legitimize his formal position; in the world of man and man, this foreman cannot. He feels the twist of inadequacy created by the union of class and ability even more because he believes that, if he really had the drive and the ability, he ought to have become a scientist, out from under, neither responsible for the drones nor to his supervisors: "If I had really developed my science, I wouldn't be involved in such a situation in the first place." We saw, in the badges of personal ability worn during a courtship, a family fight, within a school, that the actors felt personally responsible for the labels of ability they bore. But here is a man, fully cognizant of how much the corporation has defined his role for him, beyond his control, still feeling this same sense of personal responsibility. Even though he formally stands out, he feels he is still not an individual on his own. If real power corrupts, as Lord Acton once wrote, then corporate responsibility for the mass dishonors by association.

Louis Althusser's observation that class differences come out of a common root-set of problems creating "class," is all-important in understanding the tensions George Corona faces at work. He is at once, in his own mind, in control and powerless, someone who has succeeded in and someone who is alienated from the corporation, because of the hidden dimensions of individuality, ability, and unequal worth which suffuse formal class lines. It is also true that the workers below Corona, because of where *they* stand, have somewhat different feelings about themselves stemming from the same hidden roots.

To see the differences, we need first to understand a peculiar common ground shared by all the actors, regardless of their position: a common consciousness of time.

For the mass of children in the Watson School, the classroom day with its obligations to perform was not the "real time" in their lives. They thought that when they could leave the institution and get out on their own, working, then they would come alive. Adults who move into the institution of work, however, react to its demands for performance the same way the children did to the demands of school: they think about the meaningful time in their lives as the time spent outside the institution. Corona, for example, feels that "the job's just cash to live; the things that matter every day to me are at home . . . the family, people in the neighborhood." Carl Dorian, the angry young electrician, also feels absent at work. When he was in school, he says, he always thought of work as an activity in which he could "stop daydreaming"; now he daydreams at work—but what the next kind of real time is, he has trouble imagining.

Corona feels "absent" at work because he feels compromised there. Carl and other workers who have not acquired even the symbolic independence of a foreman, feel this way for somewhat different reasons. When you are just taking orders, you are not really alive, you almost cease to exist in the present, you blot it out. "What do I think about at work?" says a woman factory worker. "What can I think about? . . . you know, it is very hard for me . . . it, what can I say, I'm nothing there . . . I let my mind wander, I mean I just think about my son or like it was in the old country . . . it is very hard for me . . . just being there."

One aerospace worker pinpointed the paradox in the situation very well, in reflecting on his own daydreaming at work. The more a person is on the receiving end of orders, he said, the more the person's got to think he or she is really somewhere else in order to keep up self-respect. And yet it's at work that you're supposed to "make something" of yourself, so if you're not really there, how *are* you going to make something of yourself?

This may seem a trivial issue, but to people on the receiving end of orders it is very important. Whereas the children see the power figure as a passive audience, a judge, and themselves as performers, a more complicated consciousness of power is found among Corona's workers. The higher-ups do push people—George Corona is a prosecutor to them. Yet when they think about the meaning of time spent under his rule, they hold themselves wholly responsible for their feelings of absence at work. If they had more drive and commitment, they wouldn't feel so absent, they would make something of themselves, and yet it is Corona who tells them what to do.

94

Under these circumstances, how much a person has to take orders comes to represent inversely how much ability he has at work, for the more talent a person has, the more freedom, the more independence he ought to have in his job. This may seem abstract, as it indeed seemed abstract to us and the other interviewers when we heard people get anxious about daydreaming, because we as outsiders tended to perceive feelings in simplified either-or terms. If someone *knows* that a boss or supervisor exercises control over him, how can he also feel that being attentive on the job—which is to do good work, which in turn is a source of self-respect —is his personal obligation? The complexity of feeling here is that you can know someone else has made work boring for you by telling you what and how to produce, yet since you are acting, since you are alive those eight or ten hours, your feelings are a problem about you; *you* aren't coping. It is in this way that restricted freedom for an adult, leading to feelings of boredom or absence, restricts dignity, not because the worker feels directly oppressed but because he feels existentially responsible for the feelings restricted freedom creates.

To put this in somewhat grand terms, a person takes responsibility for his own alienation. He has to, because he isn't just a function in some behavioristic or materialistic game of chess, he is a human being experiencing that alienation day after day. There's little human reality to the philosophic resignation with which a man would "understand" that his feelings of alienation are caused by external limits on his freedom. Sartre has written beautifully on human beings' need to make sense of social life in terms of intimate experience, and what these workingpeople are saying is that the constrictions of freedom in their lives can be made sense of only by assigning a measure of inadequate coping, insufficient ability at work, to themselves.

This existential wound becomes a way for people to compare their own social position to other people's. When a janitor in a downtown office building self-disparagingly says, "You don't need no degrees to clean," he is putting himself in a different position from a master electrician who says, "I know I'm doing good work; I mean, being an electrician is nothing to be ashamed of." What separates these two is that while the janitor gets little satisfaction from cleaning, to be sure, he's not ashamed of the act of cleaning; the shame lies elsewhere. He feels if he had been "a better person, like if I made something of myself, then people couldn't push me around . . ." It is the kind of self-accusation similarly picked up in the words of a nearly illiterate garbage man: "Look, I know it's nobody's fault but mine that I got stuck here where I am, I mean . . . if I wasn't such a dumb shit . . . no, it ain't that neither . . . if I'd applied myself, I know I got it in me to be different, can't say anyone did it to me."

These feelings amount to a sense that the "lower" a man defines himself in society in relation to other people, the more it seems his fault. We saw this self-accusation in the schoolroom when a boy could feel the teacher wasn't treating him as an individual because he didn't have enough ability. Now that self-accusation in adult life gives the worker a way to label his social class; the more he must follow orders, the lower he is, because, evidently, the more he lacks the inner resources to be independent. The child accepts the shaming he experiences as legitimate, and shows his anger at the situation by attacking those who are not shamed. The adult, confronting the situation head-on, insists it isn't right society should think of him as a "nobody," isn't right because he never had a chance to be anything else. In the adult, however, there is a split between conscious belief and inner conviction—in secret he feels ashamed for who he is. Class is his personal responsibility, despite the fact he never had a chance. In one interview the janitor erupts, "So like how people, how do they know who I am? . . . I never had a chance to make something of me like you college boys . . ." The garbage man: "Never learning to read good . . . it was out of my hands . . . I mean I wanted to, but I got bad breaks . . ." The factory laborer: "There's so much in life a person has to take, things they never made, and why? I think it's unfair, I'm as good as those ladies in Saugus [a lower-middle-class suburb]."

"See, when I was growing up," said one man, "I didn't know no different, I mean who I was, I was just a kid, you know, but then I went to work at the machine shop and like, it hit me. Life, people can order you around, and you got to take it 'cause you need the job. But, it's more too, like they got a certain right to tell you what to do, okay? So it hurts, so what are you complaining about?" The anger at people who can "order you around" is confused when you also feel they have a right to tell you what to do.

Student and teacher, worker and foreman: The transposition of class from the world of childhood to that of adulthood makes the badges of ability so much more complex because the adults need to define themselves. Yet we distort the meaning of this hidden dimension in adult life if we think of these roles only in terms of separate persons. The real impact of class is that a man can play out *both* sides of the power situation in his own life, become alternately judge and judged, alternately individual and member of the mass. This represents the "internalizing" of class conflict, the process by which struggle between men leads to struggle within each man.

FRATERNITY AND INDIVIDUALITY
AT WORK

The plant where William O'Malley works is a modern, sprawling one-story building without windows, spotless within and surrounded without by a carefully tended lawn. O'Malley works on an assembly line, but the line is quiet and so much of the production is performed by automatic machines hidden under steel cases that it is difficult for an observer to believe that the men in their work shirts, their hands stained with grease, are in fact involved in making the transistors that spew forth in neatly packaged boxes.

William O'Malley grew up in a home where both parents, unskilled day laborers, worked during the day, and the father worked two or three nights a week as well. To William, his parents' exertions just to survive had bad effects on his sisters and himself. "You know, we came home from school to an empty house, so we could just run wild. I don't want that to happen in my own family." O'Malley does not permit himself to work overtime, except when the plant needs him in an emergency, nor does he permit his wife to work— although she would like to, because she feels she is "climb-

ing the walls" every day before her son James comes home
from school.°

At first, when talking about his work, O'Malley sounds
very tough and self-confident: "I have a tough job. I have to
do a number of inspections of complex machinery on this—
they call it a variable-speed line. That means when the machines can move pieces through at different speeds. I've
learned to do the checking at the fastest speed the line can
move. In the last couple of years, I got to the point in the
shop where I regulate a good part of the total line speed."

He knows he is good at his job, and he knows also that his
employers like the work he does. O'Malley believes strongly
in the virtues of hard work, not so much because it is intrinsically satisfying, but because this virtue maintains the good
home: he has kept his job in lean years, he can plan the family budget with the expectation that his income will keep
rising.

"You said, Mr. O'Malley, that you thought hard work was
really important for a man's self-respect. It seems like here
in the shop you can do that, keep the line moving, you know
. . . What effect does that have on other people, the fact
that you can do this?"

"Look, you maybe have the wrong impression of me, I'm
no slave driver about this, I just know I can do it. As long as

---

° The O'Malleys are in this regard unusual among those with whom we spoke
and among manual laborers generally. Normally, the father will take extra work
whenever he can get it, or even an extra job. But O'Malley is not as unusual in pro-
hibiting his wife from working. "It's not decent for a child to have no mother to
come home to," said another workingman. A mother who did work told us that
"My greatest fear is not about how well I do on the job—it's simple sewing, and
anyhow I don't care, I just want the money—it's what is happening to Teddy when
I'm away. As soon as Joe [her husband] is better, I'm going to stop, even if we eat
spaghetti three nights a week."

the work looks all right to the foreman, okay. Especially, because of the government contract there are a few colored men in the shop, new people, and they don't know the machines yet. Well, I'm not going to move the line any faster than they feel comfortable about. Or if a man's hung over or something—the idea isn't to press, just to turn out those transistors."

"So what do you mean by hard work?"

"Well, applying yourself, doing the best you can. You . . . in the shop you work with other people; you don't want to screw your buddies."

The more we talked to O'Malley, the more he began to wonder what in fact he meant by the words "hard work." Hard work, he decided, is more than working long hours or becoming physically tired, it involves commitment. To what? To doing a good job. What does that mean? Finally, O'Malley decided, it was a matter of doing the job in such a way that other people respect you for it; the virtue in hard work is extrinsic, in a way, to the work itself. But who is it, then, who will give you the respect?

Here the foreman intrudes. O'Malley is a skilled worker in a technological industry, and he feels he has a fair degree of independence from the foreman. "Mr. ——— [the foreman], he's a symbol you know, a figurehead." His main function is like the teacher's in school: to judge performance rather than to perform himself; his power lies not in telling people what to do, but in recommending or deciding who works well enough to get merit increases, where personnel should be placed, who should be promoted and who fired.

O'Malley is working hard, to be noticed by him. Yet because O'Malley also takes notice of the other workers around him, because he is sensitive to them, he becomes caught in a contradictory morality of craftsmanship. On the one hand, a man is supposed to do the best he can on the job, so that he gets rewards from his superiors. O'Malley has this ability, and he knows it. But, like the children at Watson School, he sees a human penalty he has to pay if he uses his ability without restraint this way. In a large shop like this, not everyone can cope equally with the tasks imposed, and the inequality in coping is not simply a matter of one man like William O'Malley being more skilled or determined. All sorts of problems and disruptions that occur in day-to-day living can intrude—a hangover, a feeling of depression after a family fight. For a man like O'Malley, it would be a denial of his own humanity to work at top speed and disregard all this; to respond merely to the dictates of authority, to work as well as possible, violates his sense of fraternity.

The result for O'Malley is that "I try to work as hard as I can without standing out, without seeming special; there's this, too—I don't want to get the other guys against me." Despite all the pressure his family values put on his success at work, O'Malley does not act there as he first presented himself. Work is not an instrument, he holds back from the individualism he feels he ought to exhibit. This desire to do the best you can, yet not to stand out so that the others are put in a bad light and resent you, does resemble the divide between achievement and fraternity generated in the authority situation of the school. But the split now has a larger dimension. Now this man is not working just for himself, he is working for others, working so that his wife can remain home, so that his son can grow and develop to lead a richer life. That is to say, if he acts strictly like an economic individual in one sphere he can strengthen his social bonds in another. Yet that balancing act won't work: he is not converted into a simple, self-absorbed economic individual on the job, because human sensitivity is not a thing a man can leave at home.

Put in larger terms: O'Malley has a formal freedom, the possible freedom of just getting as much as he can for himself, that he can't exercise if he wants to maintain a sense of his own dignity in relation to other men. To be "free," in the classic economic sense of the word, is to be reprehensible. That is the contradiction O'Malley faces in his feelings; it creates a struggle within him, a confusing set of images in his mind of who he is and what he wants.

This internal conflict O'Malley faces between hard work and fraternity is complicated also by the fact that power in his factory—in contrast to the situation in school—does not appear as a tangible person.

Neither the foreman, O'Malley, nor the other workers in his shop operate in a vacuum. In a factory, the shop works as it should when a certain quantity of goods is produced, a quantity of goods determined by authorities higher than the foreman. It is O'Malley's job primarily to make sure the machines produce enough to satisfy the demands of the foreman, who in turn must satisfy the demands of directives sent down to him. The impersonality of power in this situation affects O'Malley mainly by interfering with his ability to show fraternal feeling to other workers.

He can and does allow other workers to slow down on the job because of individual troubles they may have had at home. Yet O'Malley can only reasonably make these allowances to the extent to which he ultimately insures the production of his quota of goods. Side by side with his more human feelings towards his fellow workers there rests the necessity of treating them as a means to an end—the end of keeping the machines going fast enough to avert any risk of his losing his own job. The foreman over O'Malley is in a similar position. The faster the rate of production for which the foreman and O'Malley are responsible, the less tolerant each can be of human variations, idiosyncrasies, levels of skill, and extra-work difficulties of others.

If O'Malley just kept to himself and followed the rules, these considerations would not impose a strain on him and he would be as "tough" as he talks. But O'Malley is not a machine—that is where his inner problems begin. When one talks to this man long enough, there surfaces in him a feeling of helplessness, "in meeting the responsibilities I have . . . I can do it, I do do it—I mean, I've held this job even through the layoffs here, but I just don't feel comfortable, if you know what I mean."

"What's wrong? Try to put your finger on it."

"Well, like I'm afraid it's something gone bad in me, like I get in my own way . . ."

"What do you mean?"

"I can't explain it to you . . . it's just that I'm doing what I'm supposed to, and still I don't feel like I'm doing good enough."

The inadequacy this man feels comes to the same point as that of the child labeled "nothing special" in school: he feels responsible for a situation he never made. But the road to that point is in him quite different. O'Malley knows he has ability, but the situation in which he can use his ability is explosive. If he demonstrates his ability to the full, he stands out as an individual, not merely losing the affection of his comrades but, by becoming an example of the unusual person who is hard-working, putting them in the shade. His sensitivity to the prospect of shaming others leads him to hold himself back. But holding himself back, he makes himself feel weak. Holding himself back, in order that others not be shamed, he comes to feel he is doing something wrong. He is neither fraternal nor individualistic; he tries to be both, and feels that if only he were a more competent person, he could solve the dilemma.

It is important to recognize the limits of this conflict. The inner accusation that he is doing something wrong doesn't make O'Malley desperately unhappy; he does his job as demanded, and it is not so much a question of whether he will survive as it is the quality of his experience in surviving. That quality is revealed by such questions as who his friends are at work: "Well, I don't actually have very many *friends* here. I mean I'm on good terms with most of the guys, but it's not supposed to be a social hour, you're there to work. Actually I don't want things to get tangled up there . . . It would be messy to get to be friends with guys you're supposed to be . . . you're supposed to perform against."

Thus does the drama inside a person, between himself as an individual and as a man among men, compromise fraternity at the same time as it limits assertions of individual ability. Here is a graduate of Watson School, describing what happened to him when as a young adult in trade school he began to get interested in mechanical drafting:

"Yeah, you can hang out with the guys and have a good time—you know, who got laid last night, talk about that sort of thing—but that's 'cause everyone *can* get laid. But . . . when I started to hit the books they sort of didn't feel comfortable with me . . . I mean *I* was the same, I still liked to bullshit about getting laid, I just didn't want to stay in this lousy place driving a truck or something . . . so, I don't know, that made them kind of nervous, 'cause most of the guys have to stay right here . . . so . . . I think they kind of deserted me, but maybe they think *I* did that . . . I mean, deserted them."

And here is a civic-minded worker, who gets involved in many community, but few union, projects. Asked why, he replied that he didn't think it was "right" to get involved with people at work. Why not? "Because you're not there to make friends, you're there to get what you can for yourself."

Work is not the only terrain on which the internalizing of the terms of class occur. Indeed, the full scope of this phenomenon is missed if one looks for it only in the work realm, a traditionally masculine world. The same internalization of conflict between individuality and fraternity now marks the adult family lives of both the men and the women we spoke to; indeed, this inner class warfare helps explain another basic dilemma these white ethnic families confront, as they ponder the meaning of integration into the larger American culture.

FRATERNITY AND INDIVIDUALITY
IN THE FAMILY

The urban villages have been marked by a special kind of family—the extended family. In its simplest form, an extended family involves the presence of any relative in the house besides a husband, wife, and their children; the patterns of housing in cities make all sorts of variations possible. In Boston, three-decker houses, with either two or three separate apartments, are common. If the owner is an older person, his or her children and even grandchildren often may be found as tenants on the other floors. In cities where single-family houses predominate in ethnic neighborhoods, relatives may not actually be in the house, but close at hand down the street. All these family arrangements can be classed as extended families because they make possible extensive family contacts day to day between related groups of parents and children. Indeed, the circle of relatives often defines the circle of friends available to individuals.*

The most important thing about the extended family is that it makes the dependence of family members on each other into a code of honor. Usually this works by age, the older people having a right to set the standards for the younger; but interdependent relations occur in different ways as well. Relatives can call on each other without embarrassment in times of financial or marital trouble; child-rearing duties can be spread out; personal economic decisions like buying a house can come to hinge on all kinds of family considerations outside the individual's control. The person in this family web is seen as dependent not because he has yet to prove himself or because he is weak, but simply because he is a family member.

Historically, in industrial cities, the shelter of the extended family has been of special value to poor people. It has permitted maximum use of scarce resources, and its web

* See Richard Sennett, *Families Against the City* (Harvard Univ. Press; 1970), Chapter 4, for a more technical discussion.

helps protect individuals when they are assailed by hard times or personal disaster. The extended family, of course, is not unique to immigrant families; it is a defense that has sheltered both black and white poor in cities. It remains true, however, that this family form has been particularly well suited to the needs of the late-nineteenth-century immigrant in the decades since his arrival. In a situation where a person is largely isolated from the prevailing national culture, the extended family is a medium through which he can find immediate and sustaining bonds with others like himself.

Extended families can mean different things at different periods of history. While they allow a sharing, a mutuality, a kind of protection often unknown to persons in nuclear families, they also make possible a kind of restrictiveness, a feeling that others are always involved in one's personal affairs. What appear as sustaining bonds at one time may appear as oppressive chains at another.

Perhaps the most sensitive barometer of the cultural change that is occurring in the lives of the adults with whom we spoke is their feeling that the interdependent relations of extended families are now a source of personal humiliation rather than of collective strength. The people we encountered felt that the extended family, in this generation, has indeed become an oppressive institution. The family limits their freedom to act in such a way that they lose dignity now by following the old rules of dependence. The situation is embodied in the following angry complaint: "My father comes over and tells me the kids don't show proper respect . . . he tells me what I ought to do with their schooling . . . he's interfering, and it makes me feel bad not to stand on my own, especially in front of the kids, you know?"

The theme of conflict between generations so readily brings to mind the image of the affluent young discontented with the lives of their parents that it is easy to forget that all social history is in some sense marked by such conflicts, that the divergence between generations need not emerge only in adolescence, but in adult life as well. Among the people of Boston we interviewed, the conflict was sharper between fathers and grandfathers than between fathers and sons.

The feeling of having to get out from under the authority of their parents and relatives especially pressed on people in early middle age who were living in the same building with other relatives. One woman interrupted a group discussion on day care to say, "Look, for me this kind of child-rearing talk is off the point. Things won't get to the point where I can talk about 'rearing *my* children' until we get away from *my* folks—not that they're bad people, I don't mean that, but they know only the old ways, they want to dictate, 'cause that's what seems proper to them."

"How can my son respect me, if he sees me giving in to his grandfather, out of respect?" The young father who said this was asked if he had ever seen his own father give in to his grandmother, who lived nearby. "Now that's different, 'cause I didn't know people would ever act other than that . . . but these kids, they watch TV or their teachers, they know it isn't the same."

The "it"—the historical change this man is talking about —concerns the larger culture's assumptions about parenthood: you lose face if you practice deference as a parent, you earn respect by showing self-sufficient power, no need for aid, in your dealings with your children. Dependency, which is at the very heart of the extended family, appears as perhaps the ultimate weakness in American terms. For being dependent means you are not in control, that your actions are not of your own choosing. The acculturation of ethnic workers consists here of their coming to view as weakness the rituals that for so long—not only in American immigrant enclaves, but in many rural areas—earned people praise. The nuclear family in the suburbs, by contrast, seems a beacon of strength because it permits independence.

How has America acquired this hold over them? Is it simply that "America," the larger society, is a place of such attractiveness and warmth that the early-middle-aged parents take pleasure in leaving the old for the new? Or is there something about who the parents are, and the intrusion of class in that identity, that instills in them a compulsion to change, without real desire for the culture outside the old enclave?

That some sort of compulsion was involved appeared again and again in our talks. A young woman, echoing the feelings of others who had left their old neighborhoods, described the successful break she had made with her extended family in a move to a modest suburban home of her own: "I felt I had to leave the North End. I felt sort of that it was going to be bad for me to stay, bad for my kids . . . I think I have a better family life in the suburbs, but I'm lonely out there." Asked if she was making friends with her new neighbors, she replied she really hadn't tried, that she goes back to her old neighborhood on weekends. Asked if she liked living in the suburbs, she said that actually she doesn't, that she preferred the liveliness of the city.

A sense of loss so dominated discussions on this subject

that it clearly appeared to be more than just a feeling of temporary dislocation that would ease when people became adjusted to their new surroundings. What would they adjust to? "Here's how it is. In Boston you sit on your doorstep and ten, fifteen minutes you see ten, fifteen people you know, you find out what's going on . . . In Watertown [a Boston suburb] you sit on your doorstep, either your neighbor thinks you're funny or he invites you into his house for a drink . . . Another thing, in Boston you see a kid, you don't care who he belongs to, acting bad, I tell him to stop and if he don't I give him a whack on the behind . . . In Watertown, you take care of your own boy and you better leave the others alone. People don't want no interference."

Yet this man moved to Watertown " 'cause I wanted some breathin' room for myself and the kids—my father and mother was getting to be too much."

A number of "ethnic worker" community studies have reported sentiments similar to those described above. The old forms of intimacy appear oppressive, and you feel you have to be free. Yet when you do make the break, your loyalties and social bonds often remain with the same people as before. While you appear more in control of your own life, you feel threatened by the loss of a sense of fraternity with people you value. It can be said that an American dream of freedom, of alone-ness, has seized hold of these once-isolated people—and left them dissatisfied. But the desire for freedom is not reducible to an enthusiasm for the worldly status represented by living in the suburbs; it grows, rather, out of a belief in the concept of independence earned by ability.

Putting the connection so abstractly makes it hard to feel.

Let us give a dramatic instance of it in the ideas about family of two girlhood friends who have entered into very different adult lives.

Anna Baron and Rita Cetrulla grew up in the same neighborhood. Both their fathers were immigrant factory laborers who through many years of saving managed to buy homes. Mrs. Baron and Mrs. Cetrulla both went through the local parochial schools but neither went on to college.

Anna Baron married out of the Italian community and out of the Catholic religion. "It was a big break with my family at the time, because girls like me were still supposed to marry their own 'kind.' But Sam and I wanted to marry, and I wouldn't let my parents stop me." Sam Baron is a man from rural New England who quit school in the eleventh grade to go to work. He has been a longshoreman all his life, first a carter, now an expert handler of containerized freight.

Sam and Anna Baron have over the years healed the breach their marriage caused in her family. They live close to her parents, and see them frequently. But they find this closeness oppressive, and hope someday to move to the suburbs, or at least to another part of the city; yet they have close ties to the community socially, and are active in various local organizations.

Rita Cetrulla's marriage caused less of a stir. She married an Italian from the same neighborhood, a good match in her parents' view, because her husband was putting himself through college. Gino Cetrulla had always had an interest in working with kids, and in college he took courses that eventually led to a career as a police official working with kids. "For me, police work is a way of doing something about the conditions I saw when I was growing up. It's personally satisfying . . . I didn't want to be one of those bright Italian boys who worked their way through college and then disappeared." Gino and Rita have, however, cut themselves away from their old families. About three years after their marriage, they moved out of Gino's parents' house to a different part of the city. Although he still knows mostly Italians, they are not the people he grew up with—a fact that saddens them, but both he and Rita think it better for their own children that they have broken away.

What do the differences between these longtime friends mean? The Barons see that Rita Cetrulla, under the tutelage of her liberal, well-educated husband, has come to hold opinions on politics they have trouble accepting; but more important, she has acquired a power to make the Barons feel inadequate. When the women talk about race, for instance, Rita can make Anna feel that her fears of blacks are primitive and uncouth; when they work together in a civic improvement association, Rita can take the lead in defining what the group should do, and what Anna's role will be. Anna and Sam worry that, when the Cetrullas visit them, they will be bored, or that they, Anna and Sam, will do something wrong.

It is a socially loaded situation for the Barons. Through Rita and Gino, they are touching on a world they have not known, on a respectable middle-class life. They see that people act differently when they are middle-class, even when they come from the same ethnic background. They interpret this change not as a matter of the Cetrullas becoming strange, but as the intrusion of inadequacy in their own lives in dealing with people who were once their social equals.

How does Anna handle this tension in terms of her own family life? More generally, this question becomes: how, when you feel vulnerable in relation to people who are "respectable," do you protect yourself? There is the old way to do this, which is to withdraw into an enclave. But if, through work, schooling, and the social mobility of members of your community, and if, through the invasion of that community by the city, you can no longer insulate yourself as your fathers could, then you might try to fight that larger society on its own terms, by establishing yourself as a person anyone in America can respect—by becoming free, "your own man." If brushing against people of a higher class makes you feel open to manipulation, open to shaming, then the changes you would want to make in your life would center on matters where you do now act dependently, where you already are subject to the will of others—i.e., the extended family. That is why Anna wants to get off on her own.

But desire has not led directly to action for Anna and Sam. The deed of breaking away remains to be done. Why this holding back?

"Why don't you move if it's getting you down?" Sam Baron is asked.

"Well, it would cause the folks some grief."

"But it's causing *you* grief now."

"Well, you take Cetrulla, you know he's so advanced and all, it's the natural thing for him to do . . . now, they'd ask me why we were moving, her folks, and what could I say, I mean, by what right? If you see what I mean."

It is a mark of human beings that they need to feel a legitimacy for all their desires, not just for the power they hold. Actions based on rational calculation or simple greed are for psychology experiments; in disrupting life patterns, people need to feel worth the trouble they are causing.

The painful paradox that afflicts the Barons is that contact with the larger culture has instilled in them the desire to free themselves by turning away from the traditional family ties, while at the same time, class-consciousness makes them feel that they, unlike Gino Cetrulla, are not "worth enough" as people to be legitimate in breaking away.

Even when the break to freedom is made, if one's class remains the same the feeling of vulnerability also remains. Here is the break from the extended family in the life of a machinist, now aged twenty-eight. At seventeen he graduated from high school, "a good guy type, you know, one of the gang." His relations with his parents were on the whole friendly and close. He liked the neighborhood in which he grew up, a mixed ethnic area, established and safe. Then came four years in the Marines. "A good time in my life, you know, before Vietnam and all." The discipline in the Marines he took as a fact of military life, and it never really bothered him personally. Out of the Marines, at the end of his twenty-first year, he returned to the old neighborhood and to the home of his parents. For two years, "things are good; the old man and lady and I are getting along, they're giving me the usual advice and stuff, you ought to get married, sonny, that's all right, it was just their ways." Then he does marry, and goes from work at a gasoline station to selling shoes; now he enters on a more difficult time: "All day, 'Yes sir,' 'Yes ma'am,' I don't mind it so bad, but when I come home I don't want more of it. See, we were living near my folks and it got to me after a while. I mean, I think work made me know how the little man has got to take it, you know . . ."

INTERVIEWER: "More than in the Marines?"

"Nah, it isn't the same, like I had a family now, you know, I—I wanted to hold my head up—somewhere I think you got to take charge . . . so anyway, eventually Maureen and I moved out of the neighborhood, and I guess it's better this way . . ."

Having to "Yes sir, yes ma'am" at work makes him much more sensitive to the deference he must practice with his parents. Rather than a sustaining sanctuary, he now finds the extended family to be a replication of what he experiences at work. The move away from the family he thus sees as an opportunity to "take charge" of at least part of his life, to become in some measure "his own man."

And yet he says, "I've gone through this big change in my family, but really I can't say home is my own castle out there . . . like being in hiding . . ." What does this mean? Suburbanites are seen as people who have developed themselves enough to feel legitimate, and the newcomer therefore feels all the more unimportant.

"Um, let me try to explain to you why I was so nervous at the beginning of the interview," said a house painter. "It's not you, you're all right—but you see . . . um . . . whenever I'm with educated people, you know, or people who aren't my own kind . . . um . . : I feel like I'm making a fool of myself if I just act natural, you know? See, it's not so much how people treat you, it's feeling like you don't know what to do. Like—see, I remember, for instance, going to a

Knights of Columbus social, and there were all these people in suits and I had on a jacket, you know, a windbreaker, and somehow people were introducing themselves to each other all over the place, but nobody was introducing themselves to *me*. So that's how it is."

Not all people who leave the ethnic village in the city really leave it; many simply re-create it in suburban communities where all the other new residents are like themselves. The situation we have singled out is one in which a person or family is trying to move out of the class and ethnic confines of his past, in order to feel independent, to feel like someone "anyone else in America could respect." This phrase really has to do with those who stand higher, either the established middle-class people or people from their own background who have moved up.

We have had to talk of a rejection of the extended family in ethnic terms, for that is the past of the men and women we spoke to. Yet in the family histories of a group of workers Howard Elinson interviewed in Los Angeles, rural-born and nativist in tradition, a similar theme can be detected. Some of these workers came to the city from necessity, when their families were forced out of the great Dust Bowl territory; others came later on their own initiative to work in the city. This rural emigration to urban centers has been going on in America since the Civil War, but almost nothing is known about why it occurs, particularly among the rural young. What the people whom Elinson interviewed have to tell about themselves, however, resembles the story of the Boston workers in at least one respect: on the farm they felt that they were not on their own, that if they stayed in their parents' homes, they would be less and less in control of their lives. The farm economy has been declining for many years, to be sure, but these men were not making that calculation.

They came to Los Angeles to work in order to be free, on their own; and they feel lonely. The old rural values remain the basis for their image of dignity in social life, even as they think the city offers more occupational and material advantages. It is again a question of, when you do something to become an individual who can "take care of himself," you erode the kind of community you believe in. Like the ethnic laborers living on the outskirts of Boston, it is a matter of believing in the old values, but having left them behind in search of freedom.

The attempt to make the family independent under these conditions ends in the same kind of inner contradiction that William O'Malley feels at work. You want both the respect independence brings and the respect embodied in the fraternal bond; the contradictions between these two are insistently refracted in your mind as a matter of your own burden, your inability to make yourself appear a person "anyone else in America can respect."

Is a feeling of powerlessness at work or home similar to the feeling produced by doing poorly on an I.Q. test? We believe it is; there is a continuity in the sense of what ability means to a person, as a matter of self-perception in a world based on social inequality.

It is often said, indeed, that intellectual work has become the basis of the modern corporation—mind thinks up new things to produce, new ways to consume. We will examine the "post-industrial society" more closely later in this book; here we want only to point out that the productive image of mind cuts another way. In a wide variety of contexts where the Boston manual laborers sought to pinpoint what they might lack personally that would make them feel so vulnerable in the face of people of a higher class, it was always to notions of mind and intelligence that they resorted: "If only I were smart enough," "I really didn't have it upstairs to do satisfying work, if you know what I mean," or, "I just wasn't smart enough to avoid hauling garbage."

Are these self-descriptions true? We will have a chance later to weigh the evidence concerning good work and formal intellectual training. But the people who say these things are not really convinced these aspersions on themselves are the whole story. Mind has come to be the archetypical "commodity" men feel the need of to purchase a higher place in the social order, yet the people speaking above all feel that they have never enjoyed the freedom to really develop themselves inside—the freedom that they think middle-class people have had.

The badges of inner ability people wear seem, in sum, unfairly awarded—yet hard to repudiate. That is the injury of class, in day-to-day existence, that the people we encountered face; it is a tangled relationship of denied freedom and dignity infinitely more complex than a resentment of "what other people are doing to me." The existential problem subjects a man internally to a cross-fire of conflicting demands for fraternity and individual assertion of his own worth. How can he practically resolve these warring emotions? How does he attempt to establish freedom and dignity in the face of this contradiction?

CHAPTER II

SACRIFICE
AND BETRAYAL

In the late 1950's the Yale political scientist Robert Lane sat down with a group of fifteen men in New Haven to find out "why the American common man believes what he does." The first book to result from these interviews, *Political Ideology*, is a moving document; in part, it touches on the same conflict that has so far appeared in this book. "Most of my subjects," Lane writes, "accepted the view that America opens up opportunity to all people, if not in equal proportions then at least enough so that a person must assume responsibility for his own status." Yet subordination in social position also appears to them as the result of circumstances of birth and class, over which the people in New Haven felt they had no control.

We want, in this next chapter, to analyze what has changed in America's social structure during the last decade, so that this conflict has now assumed major proportions in the lives of workingmen. However, Lane poses a more immediate question for us to consider. He asks what kind of resolution the people caught up in this conflict try to make:

When something is painful to examine, people look away, or, if they look at it, they see only the parts they want to see. They deny that it is an important something. So is it often with a person's class status when the reference is upward, when people must account not for the strength of their position, but for its weakness.

Lane sees this feeling dealt with in three ways. A man he interviewed who said, "It's pretty hard for me to think there is anyone in the upper class and I'm not in the upper class," resolves first to insulate himself: "I have my own little unit to take care of." For an urban worker ten years ago, that was still possible culturally; there were still strong ethnic enclaves to reinforce his desire to insulate himself.

Secondly, the workers he interviewed denied the importance of the conflict itself, dismissing at various points the power of social class in their lives—even though at other times they did speak of how much class had placed them in circumstances beyond their control. Something has changed in the America known to the Boston workers we interviewed, so that we never heard the sheer power of social class dismissed.

Finally, Lane found resignation as a response to this conflict, "a reluctant acceptance of one's fate." In some cases, he noted, he was not really convinced that the pose of resignation was genuine: he could still sense a restless drive beneath the resignation; in other cases, people really did seem to deal with this conflict in the end by deciding they could do nothing.

The workingmen of Boston almost never voiced resignation in face of the injuries of class. The people we encountered had a powerful, though complicated, sense of mission in their lives: they were determined that, if circumstances of class had limited their freedom in comparison to that of educated people, they would *create* freedom for themselves. By that we mean that they were resolved to shape the actions open to them so that, in their own minds, they felt as though they acted from choice rather than necessity. It is not a question of lying about how free you are, existential philosophers have said of such resolves in general, it is a matter of thinking about your circumstances in terms of an end you choose, you want. No matter how much the world has enslaved you, in this way you keep alive your dignity as a man. The dignity the people in Boston hoped to wrest from their circumstances was expressed, however, in a paradoxical morality of personal sacrifice.

The grandson of an immigrant tailor, John Bertin works six days and two nights a week. He grosses $12,000, an amount that seems enormous to him in comparison to his parents' income, yet quite meager considering inflation, taxes, and the daily needs of his wife and five children. Mr. and Mrs. Bertin both grew up in an all-white, working-class neighborhood. In school, John Bertin barely made it through the ninth grade. "I was like runna-the-mill," he says, "the kid that didn't care. I never really enjoyed school—I hate being cooped up, I hafta be outside."

The outlines of Bertin's life form a microcosm of a development we have traced in larger terms. He felt "stupid" in school, and so came to think that his power to understand was undercut by *his* defects of character, *his* lack of perseverance, of willpower to perform well. During his earliest years, therefore, a definite connection was formed between a failure to perform for authority and a failure to develop resources of character and understanding in himself. As Bertin moved into adult life, this connection of failure in competence with loss of personal worth grew stronger; he paints delivery equipment for a large factory, people treat him like nothing. Bertin feels that his experience—his hopes, his failures, even his present struggle—has in itself no power to gain his children's respect.

He has, however, one claim on them: the fact that he is sacrificing himself, his time, his effort, for them. He has still his power to act as an agent for others, to give his wife and children the material means to move away from him. That stewardship he can indeed control. He is acting as a free man when he thinks of himself as *choosing* to sacrifice. Having been so repeatedly denied by the social order outside himself, now he will usurp the initiative, he will do the denying, the sacrifice of himself will become a voluntary act. Ricca Kartides's words return: "I am their father . . . and they *have* to respect me—because of that, and . . . because I want to do things for them." The outer face of this process is a great harshness on the part of the father; the inner face is one of self-contempt, the plea that the children not become the same as he.

Bertin's son came home from school during a talk.

"What did you do today in school, boy?" Bertin asked.

"Nothin'."

"But you were there six hours, now you must have learned something."

"Oh yeah, some calculus, some chem lab on protosyntisis, you know . . ."

"Well, that's real fine."

After his son left the room, Bertin turned to the interviewer and said proudly, "Now, did you understand any of that? Well, I suppose you did—not me. I haven't got it up here," tapping his head, "but my kids are smart—*I make 'em be that way.*"

Such fathers are determined that their children shall be very different from themselves; they do not allow the young to be indifferent about school, for it was their own failure to develop in school that has made them "run of the mill."

Again and again the fathers interviewed in Boston mixed an ideology of self-denial with assertions of their right therefore to tell children how to behave; yet these are not unambiguously authoritarian parents. "Look," said one man, "six days is a lot of work, right? Now somebody got to enjoy that, someone's got to get something from it, right?" If he is always working, his children deserve the freedom to "slack off," to be occasionally free of his discipline. He is "permissive" as long as his children follow a course that takes them from "the hard world I knew as a boy in the Depression to something decent where they can do what they want." A railroad man told us, "See, I think about that, 'specially on long trips when I'm away from home taking freight up to Maine . . . I'm thinking that's what it all adds up to now, why I spend this time away from them, because then they can take advantage of a good home."

There is a terrible paradox here, however. The "good home" can only be supported by longer hours of labor, only by the father's physical absence. But the "terrible homes" of the children of the Great Depression were curiously the same: "See, my father never played with me," says yet another man. "My father was always out, outta town, like three, four, five weeks at a time. So my mother actually brought me up, and there was only discipline with my mother; like a lot of mothers, she never hesitated to back-hand me, punch me, or whatever it was. But I think it was on accounta my old man that I want to be different in *my* life."

To devote oneself and one's life to the children has an obvious set of class limits: you must have something to give them. A destitute worker, perennially out of a job, can't feel that his sacrifices give meaning to his family life. Desperately as he may want the children to lead different lives from his own, he must struggle just to eat; everything he does concerns present survival.

Crossing that line, however, we come back to a familiar problem: isn't it characteristic of most American families, not just manual-laboring ones, to see the struggles of adult life redeemed by sacrifice for the children? A study of affluent Jewish community life, *Children of the Gilded Ghetto*, shows men who have made a go of it in business, who have not suffered the worldly constraints John Bertin knows, feeling that the strains of their jobs are also justified by the privileges work creates for their children. Indeed, the whole line of thinking about performance and respect laid out in this book leads logically to the same class-less idea: if you feel inadequate and unfulfilled in demonstrating your worth, thinking you are doing it for the good of someone else makes the performance legitimate for you. If wearing a badge of ability is alienating, wear it so that the rewards will give a person whom you love a better life.

However, class gets entangled in sacrifice in two ways.

The first is a matter of economics. A wage-worker is attempting to perform the most difficult of balancing acts: on the one hand, he wishes to be with his wife and children, to play with and show concern for them; on the other hand, he knows that the only way he can provide decently for his wife and children, and give his life some greater meaning, is by working longer hours, and thus spending much free time away from his family.

But that material calculation is not enough. Sacrifice, as an attempt to redeem the traumas in a person's life, becomes divided into unequal classes of experience. By this we mean that a working-class person has less chance than a middle-class person of sacrificing successfully; class definitions intrude to derail him from a sense that he has made an effective gift of his own struggles to someone else. To understand the inability of a working-class person to sacrifice "successfully," we should start by looking at an unspoken social contract demanded by sacrificial acts.

SACRIFICE AS A CONTRACT

Sacrificial rites in "savage" tribes manipulate time. An animal or man is sacrificed to the gods for some past misdeed of the tribe; a sacrifice is made to bring good fortune in the future; a sacrifice serves as a rite of passage for individuals in the tribe, easing them over the time of their childhood to the time of their adulthood.

Self-sacrifice in a modern family also manipulates time. To sacrifice for the children is to future-orient oneself, to delay gratification. The gratification will come when they, as adults, have moved up to a social position where anyone could respect them. Their future position will redeem the unsatisfying effort a parent makes now. Yet sacrifice in a family like John Bertin's or William O'Malley's means that the sacrificer is also making demands in the present on those for whom he is struggling.

When William O'Malley was growing up during the Depression, as we have seen, his parents were very poor, and his mother as well as his father spent all day at work, leaving the children alone to fend for themselves. For O'Malley, work is an act he performs alone so that his wife can have more free time at home than his mother had. Mrs. O'Malley, however, does not feel that her life at home is freedom. It bores her, it seems an imposition of her husband's authority. The effort O'Malley puts in at work is the answer for him to the historical conditions of his childhood; that his wife today has needs not consonant with the reparation of a wound in his past, this he does not, perhaps cannot, permit himself to see. Where he feels that by working alone he is making a sacrifice of himself *for* her, he is rather sacrificing her freedom to that wound of his past.

Men acquire status, said Max Weber, by usurpation. William O'Malley has usurped the roles of provider and intermediary to the "real" world outside the home for his family. But for a man like O'Malley this usurpation is not made without expectations. His sacrifice for his family, he believes, gives him the right to expect his family to act as he wishes; in other words, taking away their freedom is legitimate because he has denied himself out of love for them.

Sacrifice to the husband and father may thus seem here a kind of reciprocal "contract" with his family. But it is in fact only a pseudo-mutual relationship: the sacrificer does not ask his family whether *they* want him to sacrifice; the very power of this "one-way" contract lies in the fact that one person has wholly usurped the act of giving, and so prevented the others from asserting countervailing personal rights. Any accusation against the usurper is undercut *a priori* by the fact of the usurper's self-denial.

Shame, Helen Lynd has written in *On Shame and the Search for Identity,* is harder to "pass off" than guilt. When we have broken a law and feel guilty about it, being punished by others helps us make a symbolic closure to the period of wrongdoing; we are not endlessly guilty. But shame, she argues—which concerns inability, which concerns doing poorly rather than doing wrong—shame is harder to get rid of.

In some cultures, where tests of an individual come at specific points in life (tests of a man passing from childhood to puberty, for instance) a failure to perform the ritual tests well can be closed off simply as the individual grows older. Sacrifice is an attempt to deal with shaming in this most unritualistic of cultures, but the contract of rights-for-self-denial does not pass off; in Lynd's terms, there is no ritualized point the person involved reaches where he feels the shaming expunged and therefore the moral necessity for his self-denial ended.

A number of studies of the differences between middle- and working-class family attitudes point to the greater importance placed on the father's authority and discipline in working-class homes.° Furthermore, these "authoritarian" parental attitudes stretch over family time so that they are as pronounced in the babyhood of a child as they are in his

---

° The best series of studies has been conducted by Melvin L. Kohn. See his *Class and Conformity: A Study in Values* (Homewood, Ill.: Dorsey Press; 1969).

adolescence. The conclusion usually drawn is that the parent is trying to make up for his lack of status in the outer world by imposing it unendingly at home.

That conclusion is in a way true, but also in a way misleading. A middle-class father may pass off the tensions of his work by thinking he is doing it for the kids, but in the process he needn't desire that they rise to a higher class— i.e., that they become unlike him. Working-class fathers like O'Malley and Bertin see the whole point of sacrificing for their children to be that the children *will* become unlike themselves; through education and the right kind of peer associations, the kids will learn the arts of rational control and acquire the power to make wide choices which in sum should make the kids better armed, less vulnerable in coping with the world than the fathers are. If the child succeeds in becoming better armed, the father does so only by proxy: his sacrifice does not end in his own life the social conditions that have made him feel open to shame, prey to feelings of inadequacy. To call the pressure working-class fathers put on their kids "authoritarian" is misleading in that the father doesn't ask the child to take the parents' lives as a model, but as a warning.

Working-class sacrifice is not a ritual, then. It creates no closure to shame because, indeed, the ascription of weakness the society forces on men has no limits in time; the weakness is built into who they are. The contract in sacrificing is not therefore a simple transaction of, I will give myself to you, you will therefore do what I want, that will make me feel better, and I can stop feeling I have no life except through you.

If sacrifice is not a ritual, it is at least a routine. The

women with whom we spoke expect their husbands to sacrifice and provide for them, and this expectation, too, they often justify in terms of their own sacrifices as women, as wives, and as mothers. There is created in many families a kind of exchange relationship, a series of unspoken, individual expectations of obligation towards each other based on the respective sacrifices of each.

The expectations husbands had of their wives were often felt by the women to be hopelessly contradictory. The wives have to shoulder most of the work of child-raising, most of the heavy as well as light maintenance of the home, most of the shopping, bill-paying, and other clerical labor of the house. "I *can* do all these things," said one woman. "After all, that is what a man expects from a good wife. Where I feel caught is, that Eddie also wants me to be a glamour girl —I spend twelve or fourteen hours a day making the house work, and then he expects me to be sexy in bed. He says, 'If I can work hard all day and be a man at night, why can't you be a woman?' It's a whole thing about the way he wants me to act. I mean, he wants me to spend a lot of time fixing myself up and being seductive, and at the same time if I'm a good wife, I'm supposed to spend from morning to night being *the* parent and *the* bill-payer—you know, coping with life."

This divide is the mirror of the conflicting codes of love and social competence that affect young men and boys. On the one hand there is the sexual being, the "woman," and on the other hand there is the competent manager, achieving some control over the problems of running a family and a household. A woman does not appear more attractive, more sensual, more desirable in the eyes of her husband, and in her own eyes, because she can raise the children or deal with the neighbors; this ability in coping appears divorced from and in conflict with the sexual dimension.

If the women feel it impossible to satisfy adequately the demands their husbands make of them, they nevertheless often retain a profound sympathy for their husbands' burdens. This was expressed as a wish to protect the men; because their husbands were working so hard to bring home an adequate income, many wives felt they ought to cope with all the daily household cares. This was the sacrifice they felt was owed the husband, even if, as with Mrs. O'Malley, it made them deeply unhappy.

The contract implicit in sacrifice has, in sum, these lines: the sacrificer resolves to look at his own actions as essentially serving the welfare of another. Applied to children, the service is for the future; applied to either a spouse or children, the self-denial in the present legitimates limiting the present freedom of the other. Sacrifice in the home, like legitimized power in the school or factory, thus creates a conflict between freedom and self-respect.

Unlike middle-class fathers, the men we interviewed can only make sacrifices of free time. The cost of sacrifice is special also in that fathers like O'Malley and Bertin are trying, not to create a web of stability in the home, but to spur the children to develop themselves, so that they will enter a social life higher than their own.

That image of transformation across the generations gives a clue to a hidden class anger implicit in this personal resolve, beyond considerations of money and time, an image of injustice spreading beyond the home. What this transformation invites the child to do is to desert his past, to leave it

and the parents who have sacrificed for him all behind. And
if he does that, if he becomes a man of a rank where he can
command the respect of anyone, isn't he in a way betraying
them, by having risen above them? Isn't betrayal the inevitable result when you try to endow your life with a moral
purpose greater than your own survival?

SACRIFICE AND IMAGES
OF BETRAYAL

For very few does redemption come so completely as it apparently has for Tom DeWolfe and his wife. They have four
sons, all of whom respect their parents, have done well in
sports, and have been well-liked school leaders. All four
have either graduated from, or are about to enter, college.
The DeWolfes are laboring people of little formal education
who have struggled hard to provide their children with an
education and resources in the home commensurate with
what they considered the boys' abilities. "That's been my
whole life," says DeWolfe, "trying to get enough money
ahead so my boys'd get what I didn't have . . . Now my
next ambition's to retire when I'm sixty-two, so I can enjoy a
few years." They have been strict parents, requiring the
children to apply themselves and study, and have laid down
strict rules to keep the boys as much as possible shielded
from the influence of the street.

They take pride in the accomplishments of their sons, and
feel a reflected glory. They also feel that the successes of
their sons give them an edge on their neighbors, a basis for
feeling individual, i.e., superior to the other families on the
street. "There is something wonderful when you think of

how many people here alone *can't* get their boys to, you know, any type college, let alone a major college. So this is the satisfaction we're getting out of it."

Such a vicarious life through one's children, however, carries with it enormous dangers. For children are not merely extensions of oneself, embodiments of one's dreams, but themselves independent beings. What is happening in the DeWolfe family is the most direct kind of betrayal these independent beings can practice.

The DeWolfe boys, caught up in the contemporary shift in values among young people, are becoming increasingly unwilling to carry out the fantasies of retribution and justification cherished by their parents and their parents' era. They are beginning to question why they should work so hard, why they should be "Mommy and Daddy's little jewels," as one of them put it: "I look at my father and I want to cry . . . but he's getting almost to hate me because I don't want to be a lawyer or doctor or someone respectable."

As the children consider dropping out of school, or becoming artistic craftsmen, their parents worry below the surface of self-congratulation that their children may not after all redeem them in quite the way they expected. But the young who do not let their parents down also betray them.

"I always let them fear me," says Frank Rissarro, speaking of his boys in college: " 'Because you got an education under you, you gonna push me around,' I says, 'I'll throw you out of this house bodily. I don't need you.' I make them understand who is the boss and they respect me. 'Cause if I let them get away with it, they'd start, you know . . . working on me."

This is an extraordinary statement—first in its honesty, but more in the fear it expresses. Unlike DeWolfe, Rissarro *is* seeing his boys move up, fulfilling their part of the contract he has imposed on them, by staying in school. But this means they will now have power over him, will be able to "pull rank" on him and, he fears, start "pushing him around" if he "lets them get away with it."

Indeed, if the father's sacrifices do succeed in transforming his children's lives, he then becomes a burden to them, an embarrassment. A great moment of pathos occurred in our interviews when a laborer described one of the "great events of my life." This was when he went to visit his son on parents' day at the fraternity house of the community college the boy attended. His wife baked a ham, so "we have an 'in,' you know," and this was his reaction when they walked through the front door:

"I never thought I'd have my boys in a fraternity house at a university. We met some of the nicest people you'd ever want to meet. In their class and out of our class, let's put it that way. If they ever saw where I came from, the back slums of East Boston, they'd say it's impossible to even put him in our circle. I mean, let's face it, we have to be a little respectful of where we came from. That's the category he's in right now. Now he's in with a group of fellows who are educated. Now, if he goes around the corner where he came from, they're a bunch of hoodlums, hoods, period."

The destruction of respect that sacrifice most strongly creates within a home, however, does not turn on the success or failure of the young; the more direct problem is whether love can survive under contract.

The tragedy of loving as sacrifice is that those who are pushed to feel grateful cannot. Sacrifice appears to the children as a way parents have of manipulating them, rather than really loving them. The eldest son of a hard-working laborer, for instance, resents his father, and gets angry when he feels his father is "doing things" for him. He sees that it is not a sacrifice called into being because of something he, the son, has asked for; he sees it, therefore, as a hidden and rather cowardly power play by his father, a man who won't stand up for himself.

The son thus feels betrayed because his father has taken him on a "guilt trip." The father, however, also feels betrayed, by his boy's refusal to say or show that he is grateful for what the father has done. The ungratefulness of a child who has had advantages the father lacked, where the advantages were earned by the father's own sacrifices—this seems to him like ultimate injustice.

It is not so much that the father has "internalized" the values of a repressive society in his treatment of his children as that he has, rather, tried to replace the society in a certain sense, so that *he* is the one who decides to sink back to a subordinate or passive role. It is not in order to feel more debased that he makes this sacrifice. The need for dignity is a hunger pushing a person to get from day to day with the feeling that he is building some meaning, that he is adding something to the world in which he was born. That this parental sacrifice appears to the son as insidious manipulation, an imposition of a demand for blind love, is a necessary consequence neither the father nor the son can avoid.

The theme of giving oneself, and receiving ingratitude in return, stretches beyond the home to the more general awareness workingmen have of their class position in America. There is a feeling that the anxieties they have taken upon themselves, the tensions they have to bear, ought to give them the right to demand that society give something in return, that government and large institutions should not make class tensions any worse. But ingratitude is the return they feel from society, too, a refusal to acknowledge that their sacrifices finally create a claim on the respect of others.

Society's provision of welfare aid to those who do not work, is the most obvious area in which occurs this violation of the sacrificial contract.

BETRAYAL OF SACRIFICE
BEYOND THE FAMILY

"Welfare!" a bricklayer snorts. "Those lazy sluts having kids like it was a factory . . . You don't work, you don't live, right?" And yet later, talking about his oldest boy: "Why should he bust his balls to go to work, let him take it easy for a while—I've done some drifting of my own . . ."

This seeming contradiction comes from an ideology of sacrifice.

People on welfare, the bricklayer feels, have given up trying to win respect in the social order and have "gotten away with it." "I *work* for *my* money," he says. "My job is to work for my family." The sentiments are familiar; yet hidden behind them is the fact that he is tantalized by the thought of people on welfare: "They don't wanna work, they live for nothing but kicks, nothing but good booze and good sex." The image of the welfare "chiseler" is like a magnet to him; he returns to it again and again, fascinated by their refusal to make his sacrifices. "What kills me are these people that are on welfare and things like that—or like these colored people that're always squawkin'. Yet they don't wanta work. I go out, I work sometimes nine, ten days in a row, I got five children. That's what burns me, when somebody else—like this woman on the street here that collects welfare. She's a phony, but she can still collect it. She takes a cab back and forth to shop, and we pay for it."

Yet when asked directly about what it might be like to be on welfare, he answers quite differently. He knows very well that the vast majority of those on welfare are unable to work, that the number of possible "chiselers" is in fact quite small. The wife of another laborer describes how he comes home drunk four or five times a year, arguing, "It's not worth it. What's it all about? Let's go on welfare." Tempted at times by the material advantages that he believes, in moments of passion, those on welfare receive, this man is stopped by his awareness of how such people are actually treated, by the degradation he feels public assistance would bring to himself.

Why does the image of the "chiseler" so excite people? Why is anger so out of proportion to the number of "chiselers"? It is not simply because those sensitive to welfare chiselers tend to equate people on welfare with Blacks. In none of the discussions we had did people speak about Blacks as a group all cursed by heredity. The distinction manual laborers made between "good" Blacks and "bad" was that the "good" Blacks were people whom they saw living and thinking like themselves, while "bad" Blacks were the opposite—lazy, sexually insatiable, dropouts who appealed to an establishment contemptuous of the worker. While all welfare chiselers were supposed to be Blacks, not all Blacks were welfare chiselers.

A parenthesis: Much of the recent concern about discontent among white workers in America and in England has treated blue-collar workers as especially prone to feelings of racism or racial animosity, on the grounds that the challenges of Blacks press most directly on him. Careful surveys simply fail to support this notion. Racial attitudes are formed by far more complicated social determinants. Distance from a Black community, for example, is a much better indicator: those living farther away tend to fear Blacks more, since their picture of Blacks comes not through daily contact but through fantasies generated by isolation; laborers living in areas where Blacks are moving in are more prejudiced than laborers living in already-mixed neighborhoods. In one survey, the group most prejudiced against welfare "chiselers" and rioters turned out to be Black middle-class women living in Black suburbs.

It is not, then, Blacks as such that disturb the workers we interviewed, but the idea of people "getting away with something I never got away with." If there are people who have refused to make sacrifices, yet are subsidized by the state, their very existence calls into question the meaning of acts of self-abnegation. Since sacrifice is a voluntary virtue, a meaning the sacrificer has created out of the material circumstances of his life, it takes only one "welfare chiseler," getting sympathy and help from the authorities without any show of self-sacrifice, to make that willed, that created meaning ever so vulnerable. Do the "chiselers" have some secret he doesn't know about? No, that would leave him with absolutely nothing; even sacrificing himself does not give strength then. If women on welfare are free, if they can receive money from the state to support themselves and their always-present but never-seen men, then he has become superfluous as the provider for his family, his sacrifices are no longer essential to his wife and children. Yet, we have seen, only sacrifice is supposed to make a person "worth" something to those he loves.

Those who refuse to sacrifice must therefore be the incarnation of evil, the denial of *anything* a decent man does, evil not simply unto themselves, but destroyers of his own powers to believe and hope. And yet they, in their good sex and good booze, show what kind of freedom comes when you stop trying to perform. It is for this reason that hard-working fathers are both appalled and fascinated by the figure of the "welfare chiseler."

One immediate result of these attitudes is that Blacks receiving public assistance—whom most studies show to hate welfare as a way of life with a passion equal to that of employed workers—meet a wall of anger and desire for revenge. The same anger at the betrayers of the contract of sacrifice reappears, however, in another context, where the threat comes not from below, but from above.

Fred Gorman, a television repairman, yields to no one in his dislike of "lazy" people on welfare. Yet his anger is equally great toward two of his fellow workers who are graduate engineers, but could not survive the late-sixties depression in the aerospace industry. (Precipitous declines like this occur, on one account or another, to about thirteen percent of professional workers.) Why does a fall from respectability so rare as this earn Gorman's scorn?

"I just don't like people like them among us," he says. "I mean, they got education." By the ideals of personal independence to which he holds, educated men should not be changing TV tubes. He has become reconciled in his own way to his own position—"I just hack around"—but it is hard for him to accept the idea that the social order could sacrifice such men as these. Educated men are supposed, after all, to have an inner, inalienable freedom, to have developed within themselves the kind of power no one else can take away. If even they prove weak, it means there is no security, no freedom, no possibility of escape for himself or for his children; it means his sacrifices are empty of their meaning. Thus he rebels at any interpretation of these men's fate which implies that they were not in control, and insists that they must have perversely *decided* to "hack around," troubling men like himself and making them feel afraid. To have such men as co-workers, then, appears to Gorman not only as a travesty of the social order, but as a personal insult. Their decline to equality with him is a kind of betrayal.

The anger many workers feel toward students springs in part from the same root. A refusal to sit on the throne of ability and privilege appears as a personal insult to those who are denied this seat. If a privileged kid doesn't want to stay respectable, how can I believe there is any escape from my own privations? They embody the future, and the future is betraying me.

At the same time, over and over again in our talks, people expressed a great resentment against "being treated like nothing," "being treated like you was dirt," "like you are part of the woodwork." How is a man to make himself visible?

"So there's these people down the street, who act like they got no self-respect . . . I mean their kids is in rags almost and they're livin' it up . . . parties and all . . . the house is always a mess, they don't make no effort . . . Yeah, it makes me mad, 'cause you know we're watchin' our step, we're trying to make a decent home, and you get people like that, they're ruining things in the neighborhood."

The anger here is expressed by a white butcher toward a white fireman, where the two families stand equal in the world. In being angry, using the tool of his own self-discipline as a yardstick, the speaker can set himself apart from the "trash" down the street who have no self-respect. Sacrifice is the last resource for individualism, the last demonstration of competence. It is always available to you, because your desires are always part of you. It is the most fundamental action you can perform that proves your ability to be in control; it is the final demonstration of virtue when all else fails.

Sacrifice, then, legitimizes a person's view of himself as an individual, with the right to feel anger—anger of a peculiar, focused sort: In setting you off as an individual, a virtuous person compared to less forceful others, self-denial makes possible the ultimate perversion of love; it permits you to practice that most insidious and devastating form of self-righteousness where you, oppressed, in your anger turn on others who are also oppressed rather than on those intangible, invisible, impersonal forces that have made you all vulnerable.

In a way, the analysis of sacrifice and betrayal we have so far given is terribly misleading. If sacrifice sets in motion the presumption of a social contract so liable to be betrayed, then the problem might appear to be simply how people organize their consciousness. Personal therapy would seem called for, so that workingpeople would stop trying to get a feeling of personal worth, of personal right, through self-effacement.

The trouble, however, is that investing one's social position with moral meaning through sacrifice is a desire bred in its turn by forces beyond a person's control. Society is the source of this "problem," society forces men to translate social position into terms of personal worth; to arrest this fear of betrayal therefore, this fear that turns men against one another, the classification process in society itself needs to be arrested. This social genesis of feelings of betrayal we can perhaps make clearest by quoting in full, and then interpreting, the most dramatic discussion of all our formal interviews.

This talk occurred one afternoon among six women whose children all attended the same nursery school, in an all-white neighborhood populated mostly by blue-collar workers. At the height of the discussion an argument broke out between Dolly Sereno and Myra Gould about the oldest cliché in race relations: intermarriage between blacks and whites.

Dolly Sereno asked, "What would you do, Myra, if your Alice brought one home to marry? If she brought a black man home to marry?" Myra replied, "You know this"—and stopped to smile—"every bigot asks that question."

"Well, I'm asking it," Dolly replied. "I might be a bigot!"

There was a pause, and Myra began a preface to what might have been a long talk. "You know, because they feel that we don't like them—" But here Dolly cut her off and asked more sharply, "But what would you do yourself,

Myra?" And the other women began to smile and nod their heads in approval of Dolly's prodding.

Myra said, "What would I do? First of all, first of all, if you want to go into it, I'd be very happy to. First of all, my children are associated with *many* blacks—you know, in Roxbury [a black ghetto in Boston]. Okay, fine, I would not push my daughter to date . . . my children know exactly how we feel on this stand. I wouldn't particularly care for my daughter to date or marry a Negro, a black person."

Dolly asked, "Why?"

"Not because of the fact that they're black. Because of society. I wouldn't want her to be hurt by bigoted people. But I will say this: if she met a, well—I'm not sure how to say it—a black person who was like a 'beautiful' person, you know. And she took him home, I think—I hope I would have the courage. I'm not saying I would, because I don't think you can ask a person something like that, but I hope I would have the courage to be able to see this person as a human being. A person that God Himself made. And I wouldn't, you know—look, years ago, Dolly, if I brought home an *Irishman*, my mother woulda thrown me through a pane-glass window."

Dolly, whose parents were also Italian, said, "I realize this. I realize this. Yeah, but you said previous that you hope she doesn't marry [one] because of society."

"Society is ignorant, okay?" Myra replied. "Years ago, if you saw a black and a white person walking in Boston, you'd stare at them until they'd almost faint in the ground. Today it's just a matter of—you say, oh, well. You don't really think too much about it, it doesn't hit home. I don't happen to live where black people live, so that chances of my children even meeting with blacks, on that level . . ."

Kathy, an onlooker to this exchange, challenged Myra: "Yeah, but you just said they were involved with them."

Myra answered, "Oh, yeah, they know a lot of black kids, but they're not *living* with them, you know. Ask me a question like, would I mind renting to a black person or would I mind living next door."

Interviewer: "Would you?"

Myra: "I certainly would[n't mind], I'd rent to a black person in five minutes. Wouldn't bother me in the least. I would live next door to them, I would be friendly to them, I mean, I *have*—and I don't see that they're any different!"

Dolly Sereno ventured tentatively, "I—I just wouldn't want any of that . . . I'll tell you right now, truthfully."

It became Myra's turn to question: "Why? Well, tell me why?"

Still hesitating, Dolly said, "Because I just don't . . . I—" Myra interrupted her in a tone of satisfaction: "You don't think they're good enough!"

Dolly said, "Now, I'm not saying that they're not good enough, 'cause I know a lot of people that—black people that are better than some white people I know."

Myra: "Right. Okay. If your daughter brought one home—"

Dolly: "I would *die!*"

Myra: "Why?"

Dolly: "I'll tell ya the truth—"

Myra: "Why, though?"

Dolly: "I would *die!*"

Myra: "Yeah, but you can't just say you would die. You have to have a reason why you would die."

Dolly: "Because I wouldn't *want* her to *marry* a *black* person. First of all, I wouldn't want to have grandchildren from that . . . thing."

Myra: "What thing?"

Dolly: "From that union. I don't know what word I want. I wouldn't want grandchildren, 'cause those grandchildren—"

Myra: "Their skin would be black."

Dolly: "Not necessarily. Half would be black, half would be white. But . . . I would like to see my grandchildren brought up—"

Myra: "Your daughter could marry a dark Italian, you'd have darker kids than some of the black people."

Dolly: "All right, but I'm just saying . . . But it's still not a black person."

Myra: "It's a white!"

Dolly: "Right."

Myra: "That's where you draw the line."

Dolly: "You bet your life."

Myra: "Well, then, you're bigoted."

Dolly: "Well, maybe I *am* a bigot!"

Myra began to calm down and replied almost to herself, "Well, that's the first thing you'd have to say." At this, Dolly looked hurt: "I mean, I know what you're saying—but you yourself wouldn't . . . don't say you're not gonna . . . you wouldn't *die* if Alice brought—"

But here Myra commented almost distantly, "No, I wouldn't die"; and suddenly Dolly erupted, shouting at Myra with real scorn, "Oh, Myra, don't say that!"

Dolly Sereno later remarked in private conservation that what made her so angry was Myra's refusal to admit that her own feelings were like Dolly's, Myra's "putting some-thing on." And when we spoke individually to the other women, they reacted the same way. They sided with Dolly because they thought Myra was "striking a pose," was trying to "put them down." Myra's private feelings about this argument fitted the opposite side of the mold. To her, Dolly, whom she liked and respected, was "acting in a silly, unthinking sort of uneducated way."

In this conversation, a hidden, silent authority—the inter-viewer—had a kind of magnetic pull on Myra: it was at the interviewer that she often looked while she was ostensibly speaking to Dolly, seeking approval for her enlightened views. One of the other women later observed that they had never known Myra to talk this way privately. The change was not so much in her beliefs, Kathy said, as in the manner in which she spoke, the eagerness with which she forced Dolly to announce herself as a bigot. The other women felt betrayed by Myra, seeing her as "putting something on" in an effort to differentiate herself from the rest.

In fastening onto the interviewer's presence, in per-forming for the outsider to show that she too was educated and "enlightened," Myra had brought to this discussion the weight of a whole lifetime of experience that made her feel obliged to prove she was "worth something" to those "above" her.

The pattern of such a lifetime experience of proving one-self, the need to separate oneself from the mass which we have explored so far in this book, gives to political issues a distinctive texture and form.

The people in the group around Myra believed she was arguing for the "right" thing, the enlightened and educated thing, just as they believed she was saying the morally right and educated thing when she condemned the war in Vietnam, hunger in America, and the like. But she makes them have a problem with that content. For while her words denote love of mankind, they connote shaming and rejection of *them*. Since Myra is emphasizing these opinions to gain the approval of an outsider whom she sees as upper-class and educated, and in so doing to stand out from the others, the other women cannot help but question the sincerity of her sentiments, because she is not being considerate of them. If she is really so tolerant, why does she use her tolerance to betray them?

In the argument between Myra and Dolly, another dimension comes into play. When Myra says Dolly is acting in a "silly, . . . uneducated way," she is shaming Dolly by trying to put her into a mass, so that Dolly disappears as a person in front of her, talking to her right here and now. The whole idea of the "hard hat"—the superpatriot, the racist workingman—serves the same purpose: a hard hat is a thing, with an empty head hidden beneath, a part of a mass over which the "educated" or "enlightened" person towers. The postures of enlightenment and civility become, in the magic mirror of class, the means for an individual to make a crowd, in the same way the teachers at Watson School make a mass out of the persons in the classroom. Class creates fratricide in this scene; class provokes a desire for personal recognition in Myra and a feeling of betrayal in Dolly.

Personal sacrifice intervenes in, but does not create, such a destructive force. Take, for example, Michael Bowers, a young man recently returned from Vietnam. While there he came to detest the war he was fighting; but he says that the more he came to hate the war, the more he came also to hate the war protesters at home: "They're your real suburban liberals, those people. They think they can sit in judgment on what other people do. I had to fight over there . . . I mean, I grew up with all the patriotism, the VFW crap, and like, it *hurt* to change, I went through hell . . ." The war protesters are spoiled because they make moral judgments on others without going through that hell. "Their advantages, you know, wealth, education, the suburbs, all that, make them think they can be more moral. They can understand *you*, with all their fancy words, but you can't understand them, 'cause you're just a part of the scenery. Well, actually nobody can understand them, they think, you know, 'cause they each got their individual problems, their shrinks, they've always been special." No one can really "understand," in the way Bowers has come to understand, the meaning of war just by sitting back and analyzing. Yet the elite who have developed their minds think that, with their expertise, they need not get involved in order to understand.

In both cases, in the argument between Myra and Dolly, and in the expressed feelings of Michael Bowers, the overt issue is but a cloak for a class antagonism. Those against the war did not set out to make Bowers angry—quite the reverse. Nor did Myra Gould set out to make Dolly Sereno angry; she only wanted to win the approval of an outside authority, the interviewer, and became blind to Dolly's feelings in the process.

The terrible thing about class in our society is that it sets up a contest for dignity. If you are a working-class person, if you have had to spend year after year being treated by people of a higher class as though there probably is little unusual or special about you to catch their attention, if you resent this treatment, and yet feel also that it reflects something accurate about your own self-development, then to try to impugn the dignity of persons in a higher class becomes a real, if twisted, affirmation of your own claims for respect. Class, in the terms of this book, class as a problem of day-to-day existence rather than as an abstraction, creates a hidden content in a wide variety of social issues, so that while people like Myra and Dolly seem to be fighting over general principles, they are in reality fighting for recognition from each other of their own worth.

Class politics are too complicated at this level to assign blame to either side. War protesters and middle-class radicals genuinely mean well—so does Myra. In this fight she was truly afraid that her friends were trying to "drag her down" to their own level; she knows racism is wrong, and Dolly's claims to equality made her ashamed in front of the interviewer. Even so, she needs peers like Dolly, she needs them in order to stand out from them.

The Enlightenment philosophers told us that human dignity is a possession of all men, that there exists what they called "common humanity." In a society which professes belief in this ideal, yet which is also arranged as a set of hierarchical classes, to assert the humanity you share in common with all men can move you in two directions. In the first, you make an effort to place yourself on a par with those you believe to be above you; in the second, you attempt to destroy inequality between yourself and the persons you perceive above you by attacking their integrity.

Let us tie this general idea to the myths of individualism

in our national culture. We have long celebrated the individual as a hero because he has been, as portrayed in our literature, and more recently in our movies and television, alone in being specially honest, or courageous, or true to himself. But to celebrate individualism in a class society has a perverse, if unintended effect. In such a society, the moment individuals are praised, subterranean fears of betrayal and shaming are set in motion. The war between Myra and Dolly, the resentment Bowers harbors towards people united with him intellectually in opposing the war, these are the logical products, the necessary images of desertion, that flow from the conflict between brotherhood and achievement in the Watson School, or in the adult situations faced by Carl Dorian and William O'Malley. What is one person's individual achievement in the eyes of authority becomes betrayal for the others.

For the betrayed, what is the alternative to individualism? You assert a common humanity, equality, you desire to get those who are in higher social positions to admit the worthiness you share with them, you want them to stop treating you as an object. But what if you believe that your social position is your own burden, a matter of your character? How then can you legitimize such an assertion of equality?

Michael Bowers does not feel illegitimate in his anger at suburban liberals, and the reason is that he sacrificed himself in a war. Like John Bertin, he legitimizes himself through his acts of sacrifice. With Bowers, this self-legitimization extends beyond the family but operates along the same lines: because Bowers denied himself for his country, he now feels the right to condemn individuals in it.

Work and warfare move to the same end: the more they make a man feel he has denied himself for the sake of others, the more right he feels he has, not to submit to the moral domination of anyone else. The feeling of having acquired the right to equal dignity, is, however, complex. Neither Bertin nor Bowers nor Myra is thinking about doing away with the class structure. They, too, are individualists, concerned with their right to be exempted *personally* from shaming and indignity. In turning people against each other, the class system of authority and judgment-making goes itself into hiding; the system is left unchallenged as people enthralled by the enigmas of its power battle one another for respect.

CHAPTER III

THE USES OF
INJURED DIGNITY

A reader mindful of how this book began might now criticize it for drawing a condescending picture of workers afresh. At the beginning, the authors had harsh words for radicals who despaired over "false consciousness" among workers, who dismissed workers for being bought off or gulled by the "system." Yet aren't sacrifice and betrayal, the search for dignity through validation of the self, the interpretation of freedom in terms of inequality of talents, aren't all these psychological themes matters of false consciousness? People believe in these ideas, act or react in terms of them in daily life, even as the psychological images are destructive to both personal dignity and freedom. If people had "true" consciousness, wouldn't they stop believing that they could validate their dignity through sacrifice, for example, wouldn't they realize how they are being manipulated?

We think this is a serious objection to where we've come compared to where we started. We would like to begin to meet it by remarking on a phenomenon that may seem at first glance to be beside the point. In our presentation of class injuries thus far, we have described an experience, an existential problem of freedom and dignity; but we have not explained *why* society has created that problem.

In the classroom, in the shop, the figures in charge bring assumptions about class and ability into face-to-face dealings with their charges. But where do these assumptions come from? In describing the inner conflicts of a hard-working skilled laborer, or of someone trying to break away from an extended family, we have shown how power of the need to demonstrate ability is "set up" in people's lives so that they feel *a*, *b*, or *c*. Who or what did the setting up? Validating the self through distinctive personal merit is not a matter of spontaneous desire; if O'Malley, Rissarro, Kartides, and the Barons really had their choice, they wouldn't want to try proving themselves for the sheer pleasure of it.

These questions about experience suffice to show that there must be some compulsion, some magnet, from the larger society that enters into and gives form to people's daily experience. The people who have appeared in this book would have a "false consciousness" of themselves if they misinterpreted the nature of this magnet, this compulsion. It is of course impossible to judge, merely by listening to people's experience, its "truth" in terms of what society is "actually" doing—that is the great limitation on a book of interviews. However, in talking to these men and women, we found nothing illogical in their language, no disunity in their perceptions; they seem, in fact, to act almost too rationally in confronting the dilemmas they feel have intruded from the larger society into their lives.

Yet we cannot help wondering about the kinds of social forces which shape the experience that people have, but of which they are not conscious. In particular, a devil's utilitarianism has dogged us in speculating about the source of these feelings: what purpose does demonstrating one's ability serve, what use is it to society? The question assumes that American society "benefits" when it makes people feel anxious, defeated, and self-reproachful for an imperfect ability to command the respect of others. The use we see in general, which we shall try to show in the following pages though we cannot prove it directly through interview material, is that society injures human dignity in order to weaken people's ability to fight against the limits class imposes on their freedom. We do not mean that the men and women we encountered were ignorant of the fact that class conditions limited their freedom—it is palpable from the interviews that they do know this. Rather, the use of badges of ability or of sacrifices is to divert men from challenging the limits on their freedom by convincing them that they must *first* become legitimate, must achieve dignity on a class society's terms, in order to have the right to challenge the terms themselves.

SCARCITY OF REWARDS

In a study of auto workers on the West Coast, Bennett Berger found in a typical factory that six foremen's positions became open over the course of some years for three thousand workers—the ratio of foremen to workers being one to several hundred. Yet the foremen's jobs were much sought after; more than fifteen hundred of the three thousand workers wanted one of the six openings for themselves.

The company, to keep those fifteen-hundred-odd ambitious men hard at work, has to find a way of making this reward believable, in the face of the fact that it must deny at least 1,494 of them promotion over a reasonably long period of time. Say only one in ten of the aspirants meets the most stringent requirements; there will still be 144 or more unaccepted acceptable applicants for the six places. How is the company going to keep its best men content under these conditions?

This dilemma embodies a classic contradiction between a scarcity of rewards and the claim of careers open to anyone of talent made by owners like Andrew Carnegie. Put another way: the promise of America for the laboring man, Samuel Gompers believed, is the promise of someday no longer having to work with his hands; anyone who really tries can wear a white collar or own a small business. This dream, however, does not bear up under the scrutiny of social research. According to figures presented, for example, by Duncan and Blau in their superb *American Occupational Structure*, if a person's first job had no bearing on where he was likely to end up in the occupational structure, fifty-two percent of those who began as manual laborers could be expected to end up in white-collar jobs; thirty percent actually do. Similarly, if the occupation of one's father had no bearing on where one would end up, the statistical probability is that forty-three percent of the sons of manual laborers would get white-collar work; thirty-four percent actually do.

How, then, is the believability of the reward system to be maintained? Badges of ability are a good measuring device in a society based on inequality, because distinctive ability

The Sources of Injury

seems to belong only to the few. But in this classic kind of
scarcity situation even ability criteria produce more eligibles
than can possibly be rewarded.

It is at this point that injured dignity serves a purpose, in
maintaining the legitimacy of a reward system that cannot
deliver on its promises. We would like, before explaining
the connection, to make clear that we see no individual dev-
ils in this devil's utilitarianism; that is, we don't imagine an
employer sitting by the pool at his country club musing on
how he can protect himself by making his workers feel inadequate.

Modern personnel managers, Sudhir Kakar writes in his
study of Frederick Taylor,* learned from the mistakes of
Taylor's "scientific management" never to judge the future
potential of an employee simply by efficient past performance. The potential for doing a higher-level job is not indicated by how an employee performed one past task; as a
textbook on personnel management puts it, the employer
has to use his intuition, to look beyond the "track record,"
to make good promotions.

This value placed on personality and intuition has a humane sound to it, and yet it helps the employer out of this
impasse of having more qualified employees than he can
hope to reward. For now he can go beyond objective or
clearly definable standards of judgment, standards he may
have himself established, and escalate the qualifications for
promotion to a mythic level beyond a subordinate's power

* Sudhir Kakar, *Frederick Taylor: A Study in Personality and Innovation* (Cambridge, Mass.: MIT Press; 1970), a fine study in this field.

to grasp. If he has only six places to offer 150 whose past performance makes them deserving, then he "intuits" which of these who have done well in the old spot will succeed in the new. Power in the organization, like the God of Weber's early Protestants, knows about you what you do not know about yourself. The hierarchy's inability to make good on rewards is converted in this way back to a question of who is worth rewarding; the legitimacy of power in the auto plant survives only as the powerful can be so very personal.

But what makes the employer's face-saving acceptable? What hope have these humane management experts from the Harvard Business School that they will be believed by all the eligible men?

It could be said that the process is believable because those in authority are sincere. Once one puts away images of employers as scheming-capitalist-demons, it could be argued that the employers believe naturally in what the structure of their organizations demand: they do want to be humane; and the workers respond on the same terms. After all, in the Watson School, the teachers did not start out hoping to wound their students, but to do some good with a seemingly unpromising group of kids; the kids responded by believing in the teacher's good faith, and feeling inadequate. Only by attacking the few favored kids did the mass of the denied give vent to a feeling that anything was wrong.

But now we are talking about a matter of ten or twenty years of hard work suddenly running up against a judgment process that changes the rules when the rewards are due. This should be the recipe for revolt.

It is the intuitive approach that saves the day here: the foreman or employer says, in effect, that there is a mystery in you; how adequate your performance is, you yourself are incompetent to judge. What is in you that commands the approval of others? You can't know this, but someone can. In talking to older laborers who worked in large factories, we often heard them express anger about how unfair it was that they—good, solid workers—had not been promoted; yet that anger was often turned around by final statements like "they must have their good reasons," or "they know what they need" to describe superiors' behavior.

Wearing badges of ability to earn love or friendship is self-defeating, because love cannot be earned. Transpose that self-defeat to the factory world: to get a reward *you* have to show you have ability, but rewards come for mysterious reasons that transcend any consideration of what you can do. Reward by intuition is believable when the denied workers feel *they* have taken responsibility for what happens in the situation, by trying to win the reward at all. The two workingmen quoted above risked themselves; like the kids in Watson School, they felt that they were performing before an authority sitting in judgment. Why did they not get approval? Like the teachers in the school who do not verbalize their distance, the employers act on nonverbal, intuitive grounds: you tried, and your performance was not condemned; you simply failed to be noticed.

The issue here obviously transcends such matters as promotion. In a class society, there are any number of vital matters in which people at the bottom are denied, even when they play by all the explicit rules for reward, or where they are burdened unfairly because of their position in the society. In our discussions, matters of urban renewal, taxation, and the war in Indochina stood out to people as such unfair burdens: urban renewal destroyed their neighborhoods, while it rebuilt the neighborhoods of Blacks, who did not struggle to maintain their homes as well; taxation for urban services fell more heavily on them than on suburanites who benefited from those services; the war took their children, rather than the college-age children of the affluent. In all these respects, class appears to them to give them less freedom than others.

Yet beneath all these complaints there lies an acceptance of the denying authority. The acceptance is on the same terms as is that expressed by the workers who describe the plant management as "having their good reasons." An interview with a man whose street was being demolished to make way for the expansion of a Boston university stands out to us. "I know," he said, "the university doesn't really need this land." He had done much work in figuring out exactly how many parking lots the school had that could be used for new buildings, and where land existed elsewhere in the area that could be taken without driving people out of their homes. In the midst of explaining this to the interviewer, he suddenly stopped himself and reflected, using almost the same words as the factory worker, "Well, they're educated people, they must know what they are doing . . . maybe there are things about this I don't know." In talks with people about the war in Indochina, that response has become familiar. The people in Washington must know something we don't know, and therefore they have some right to do what they are doing, even though from what we see, it makes no sense. (Concerns about taxes, to balance the picture, were not passed off in this way.)

For the man being displaced by the university, the people

upset about their sons drafted for the war, as for the factory workers denied promotion, the "higher knowledge" of those in power creates at once the mystification of power and its legitimacy. The apportionment of mind and knowledge represents the divide between those who judge and those who are on the receiving end of judgment; it is a charged situation that results in a sense of inadequacy, on the part of those who are being denied, to intrude upon the realities of denial they experience.

This is why worker "authoritarianism," as Lipset talks about it, is all wrong: the man who is displaced by Harvard or the people whose sons are dying in the war do not believe that whatever authority does is right. Rather, a sense of self-doubt intervenes to make them unsure *they have the right* to fight back. Is it any wonder that they often lash out, as did the kids in the school, at those who receive the unfair rewards, feeling cowed as they do in the face of the rewarder?

A class society, Sartre has remarked, is a society of scarce resources unfairly distributed because some have arbitrary power. The situation here is one where the psychological dimensions of class serve a purpose in legitimating deprivation, unfair allocation of resources, and paltry rewards.

The issues with which this book began, however, are not scarcity issues. Frank Rissarro, James, the young men whose parents laid bricks and who themselves are junior sales managers, all have received substantial material rewards; and still the language of self-doubt intrudes into their lives. Evidently, plenitude and material abundance do not erase the hidden injury of class. Why does it persist? What is its role in a situation of abundance?

DESTRUCTIVE REPLACEMENT

In the Gilded Age of hundred-thousand-dollar dinner parties and the importation of French châteaux block by block to Chicago, Thorstein Veblen wondered if the meaning of this conspicuous consumption was solely that the American rich were experts at making money and savages at spending it. He wondered what it meant to a candy-store owner or an office clerk when he read that the lobby of the Savoy in London was flooded one night and guests ate in floating gondolas imported from Venice for the occasion.

Veblen ultimately decided that the meaning of these excesses, indeed the reason they were given such publicity, was that they created a peculiar idea of affluence for rich and poor alike. Of course the candy-store owner was not going to flood his store for a family *bar mitzvah,* but he was going to believe that enjoying oneself was essentially a matter of *wasting* things, or money; you had a good time, a really good time, when you used money for something arbitrary, for excess.

There is a demonic quality in this phenomenon. Conspicuous consumption is essentially a destructive act: it destroys, in the name of pleasure, the virtues of self-restraint and moderation a man of talent is supposed to exercise in earning the money. It thus reflects a hidden hostility to the value assigned to things by the productive order; the openhanded liberality at night denigrates the worry about getting your money's worth that dominates the business day. The hostility suggests, moreover, how little gratifying the productive activity is in itself—if it were more so, conspicuous consumption could not exist.

Conspicuous consumption on the part of the rich sets the standard for all the people in a society. It tells all not what to enjoy, but how to enjoy. The more foolish, the more senseless, the extravaganzas of the rich, the more appealing as a metaphor of destruction they become for people below, who can never conceivably practice such waste.

Veblen's probing of the emotional crosscurrents of affluence has been overshadowed in the last few decades by a more glaring economic injustice. The economy each decade grows more affluent, it is true; two cars for every family, a television set for every eye. Except that the plethora of goods is not distributed in this even-handed way; the richer get proportionately more, the poor less; wealth flows more easily into the private sector than into the public—where government might use it to right the balance. What has gone wrong? J. K. Galbraith argues, in *The Affluent Society*, that the problem is essentially a matter of distribution; the public sector must get a hold on the output of goods and services, and direct distribution to right the balance between rich and poor. How things are produced, in Galbraith's scheme, is rather less important than who gets what. (Galbraith has since modified this phase of his argument in respect to the military sector.)

Production and distribution of civilian goods cannot be separated, the Marxist economists Paul Baran and Paul Sweezy argue in their book *Monopoly Capital*. Indeed, the system of economic life that produces an aggregate affluence of goods and services actually demands that the goods and services be distributed unequally.

Affluence, Baran and Sweezy maintain, is a matter of constantly expanding production through the making and remaking of standards of comfort. Once everyone, or at least the great majority, has enough to eat, a place to sleep, and other necessities of survival, the factories can stay open at all only by allotting goods and services unequally to a few, who appear more comfortable than the rest. Since these goods and services are purchasable, the people below work to consume more in an effort to narrow the margin of inequality in enjoyment of comforts; the factories then produce for mass demand. As a result, however, those at the top get still more goods and services, or new ones, and the cycle begins again. The survival of the industrial production system thus depends on the unequal allocation of affluent resources; to redistribute the flow, you would have to change the nature of the source.

This is a neat formulation, more convincing than Galbraith's analysis of why affluence continues patterns of inequality. A human element is missing, however. A man who goes into debt to buy a second car doesn't do so thinking it is his obligation to keep the capitalist ruling class in power. To say that he is envious doesn't explain why he is so. To say advertising or public-relations propaganda tricks him into thinking he needs more and more is condescending and still doesn't account for his receptivity. (To their credit, Baran and Sweezy stick to economics, and prefer an unanswered question to a glib explanation of motivation.) What is stimulating the ordinary person to play? Deducible from Baran and Sweezy's approach is an idea of destructive replacement: the present things or services one consumes are destroyed, to be replaced with new things and services at a higher level of comfort. There is something in this akin to the destructiveness Veblen saw embodied in conspicuous consumption; in both cases, man as consumer overturns his gains as producer. But the idea of destructive replacement is *self*-destroying too. Whatever plateau of material circumstance a person achieves seems to him inadequate by comparison to the comforts of people who stand higher; he wants to be like them, and so he moves on to consume more and more. The vision of an inadequacy in one's "standard of living" suggests that perhaps the class psychology we have been describing might be at work here. The constructions of class and personal worth we have traced might serve a purpose in motivating people to consume through destructive replacement.

By holding both a full- and a part-time job, Dan Bertelli, a factory worker, makes about $10,000 a year. He is knocking himself out to meet the payments on a small house and on a large Pontiac sedan. He spends almost no money on himself: "I feel guilty if I give myself more than two beers, sometimes. Well, sometimes I figure, why not go ahead and drink." He would like to spend more on his wife, give her nice clothes, but she too resists, feeling the money shouldn't be wasted on herself. The Bertellis spend a lot on family leisure, however, and are prepared to spend a great deal for their kids, rubber rafts, a little cabin on Cape Cod for weekends in the summer—weekends Bertelli works over so that the kids can get out of the city. Now he is contemplating a small boat and outboard motor so he can go fishing with his boy. It's not for himself; he echoes the sentiments of Ricca Kartides, the immigrant janitor: "It's not I want these things for myself, it's that I want the family to enjoy."

Some of Bertelli's expenditures fit a straightforward idea of how possessions can appear to make up for a feeling of personal powerlessness—his car, for instance. Asked why he didn't get something cheaper, he replies, "Because you can really move in it, you got plenty of power. In that little car of yours [the interviewer's Volkswagen station wagon], you got no control, you gonna get pushed around on the road."

But this straightforward idea of motivation doesn't explain why, in listening to a man like Bertelli, one senses that consumption for him is on the whole not a matter of pleasure, why he feels "guilty spending money on myself."

In the last chapter, we tried to show how the outcome of feeling personally inadequate was the resolve to sacrifice for others, especially for the children, so that they might someday lead a better life. This resolve, however, leaves a man vulnerable: for sacrifice to work, the recipients have to express a gratitude so humiliating as to be seldom forthcoming; and when sacrifice does lead to a different life for the young, they also leave the sacrificer behind. Sacrifice also leaves a man like Bertelli vulnerable to the power of destructive replacement.

Sacrifice turns a man toward the future. In the future, people he loves will be different from him, they will have different needs and desires; he becomes vulnerable, say, to sales pitches for encyclopedias a salesman has told him his children will need "someday." Moreover, what is true for his children becomes true for himself as well. When through the process of economic expansion new symbols of comfort among the well-to-do replace old ones—two cars instead of one, a speedboat, a personal set of encyclopedias for his kids—he is hard-put to resist the admonitions to buy, because all these objects may be necessary for someone to live a "really" respectable life, and he isn't at that point yet. It becomes credible to Bertelli that he should buy what this new, future self would like rather than spend for such present pleasures as a daily round of drinks at a bar. It is plausible that he should buy a home of his own so that his kids can play on their own turf, even though he has to work such long hours to pay for it that he seldom sees his children awake. The dream of the future, enacted in one's own life as self-sacrifice, thus makes a man yield to rather than resist the productive order putting him in a vulnerable position in the first place.

Class makes people conceive of themselves as spectators, rather than as people gratified by new material goods. When Bertelli wonders what his family should have in order to live decently, he sounds like a man who is waiting, who doesn't know when he is going to cross the magic barrier beyond which he will receive the respect of "anyone in America" for what he has done for his family. When a young Vietnam veteran driving a cab, a man with a wife and no children, talks about driving a second shift so that he can buy a little shack in the woods one day, he too is thinking of consumption in sacrificial terms; his time with his wife he will restrict now, so that someday they can go away together "where no one can get at us." When Sam and Anna Baron dream, like Ricca Kartides, of a home of their own so that they can feel independent, they are buying what they don't need for sheer survival, and sacrificing pleasures in the present so that someday their children can grow up free.

Now, it could be said that this vulnerability to pressures to consume beyond the needs of present survival, generated by a sense of sacrifice for an unknown future, that this erosion of pleasure through consumerism stretches across all social classes in society. In general this may be true; but a peculiar shift in the history of working-class consumption, as well as an insecurity in the way blue-collar income accrues, puts workers in a special position.

In nineteenth-century Newburyport, Massachusetts, a study of manual laborers showed that they would often sacrifice the possibility of white-collar jobs for their children in order to buy a house for themselves.° For the sake of this "horizontal mobility," parents would take their children out of school as soon as the young were able to do manual work. There has been much debate among historians about how commonly children's futures were sacrificed in this way during the last century. What is certain is that this sacrifice of the children no longer prevails. A wide variety of studies show that today manual laborers want desperately to give their children occupational mobility through education, even as the acquisition of a house remains a compelling dream.

It may be said that this double wish shows the rising expectations of workers in modern times, a double dream that is to be wrung from the wages the worker earns, and so strains his finances in relation to his desires. But there is also a continuity from the past here—both homeownership and sacrifices for the sake of the children's education involve delayed gratifications. The laborer must wait years for both these things, saving conscientiously. These dreams can become realities *only* if he can routinely put away money

° Stephan Thernstrom, *Poverty and Progress: Social Mobility in a Nineteenth Century City* (Harvard Univ. Press; 1964).

beyond bare subsistence needs, planning that at so much a month saved for ten-fifteen-twenty years, he will have a down payment on a house and/or college tuition for his children.

The routine, however, is harder for wage-earners to maintain than salaried office workers. Because they worked by the hour, the people with whom we spoke experienced striking fluctuations in their incomes. Thus, a craftsman's annual earnings went from $11,000 to $7,880 to $9,000 to $14,000 to $8,000, depending on how much work and overtime he could get; a factory laborer's income fluctuated between $6,000 and $8,000. Changes like these occurred, moreover, during the years 1963 to 1968, a period of steadily mounting prosperity in the country as a whole. Even those few laborers on fixed yearly wages often relied on part-time jobs to provide the savings for the delayed gratifications of house and college, and such jobs, as S. M. Miller and Pamela Roby have pointed out in *The Future of Inequality*, are the most unstable income-producing work in the economy.

What happens as a result of this divide between the reality of income fluctuation and how a person wants to use his money? The people we talked to got angry at the corporation or the government when recession times hit wages. But their intentions for the use of their money exist in another time as well, in a future where government and corporation may or may not exist, but in which a man will own a house and his kids will graduate from college. The government may be ruining him, but knowing that and complaining about it aren't going to help him keep alive and on the disciplined schedule. *He* has to do something, his very goals demand it. No one else is going to discipline him to save money. And even when times are good, the pressure is on him; his income, now touching the margin of existence, now offering a goodly surplus, becomes a perpetual burden.

"Now the trouble with you college boys is you don't know the value of money," says a typesetter. "You just don't know what it's like to save . . ."

"Well, are you hurting badly now for money, you mean?"

"Sure . . . let's see, with a little overtime and stuff on the side I make $12,000, which is okay, well actually I was only making about seven thousand a few years ago, but I just can't control the outgo, the taxes, the kids need this they need that, there has to be money someday for school . . . the more I earn the farther behind I seem to be, money's something that's just out of my hands to control, you know?"

"You going into debt?"

"No, I just can't put anything away . . . day to day eats it up . . . and, sort of what *I* want to spend money on, I got to wait, I don't know . . ."

Consumerism oriented to the future thus increases the sense of uncertainty about the self's present needs. Earning money gives a person little sense of immediate gratification —that's not what it's intended for—and little reinforcement year after year to his belief in his own power to cope. Money may someday make a man feel he has accomplished what he wants; but "someday" does not make him feel stronger now.

In *One Dimensional Man*, Herbert Marcuse has written:

If the worker and his boss enjoy the same television program and visit the same resort places, if the typist is as attractively made up as the daughter of her employer, if the Negro owns a Cadillac, if they all read the same newspaper, then this assimilation indicates not the disappearance of classes, but the extent to which the needs and satisfactions that serve the preservation of the Establishment are shared by the underlying population.

This formula misses the actual experience of workers like Bertelli or Kartides in one important respect: they do not consume out of a desire for gratification, they do not consume even with the idea of satisfying present needs. Something much more convoluted dictates their spending, something beginning with a profound self-doubt they want to resolve. If it is apparent to the observer that these modes of consumption "serve the preservation of the Establishment," that a devil's utilitarianism is involved here, it is no less true that Bertelli and Kartides think of their spending as someday giving them weapons of defense against the Establishment, weapons to defend their dignity.

Destructive replacement is more than a process of consuming; it is also the corrosive power in the great American dream of dignity through upward mobility.

MUSICAL CHAIRS

Let us say William O'Malley is promoted to chief foreman. The front office knows he can deal with the machines better than anyone else in the shop; he is hard-working, and a long-term employee. On the first day in his new job, O'Malley comes in to face the problem of one of the linemen slacking off on the assembly line. O'Malley knows how to do that job, and he knows the lineman knows how to do it, too. But his old skills are no help to him in his new role, beyond telling him this man is a problem. The arts of cajolery, threat, and personnel management are needed now, but nothing in O'Malley's past work experience has prepared him to exercise them. What he is good at he no longer does. What therefore does his promotion, his success, really mean?

This question appears in real job changes again and again; a promotion can increase feelings of illegitimacy, by destroying the present meaning of skills built up over many years. To move up and feel less secure: the mobility is a form of abundance, another step beyond sheer survival, and yet it can prove as self-abnegating as future-oriented consumption.

The reason why this contradiction would occur for O'Malley is straightforward: a skill is displaced. The contradiction could be resolved in time, when O'Malley learns the ropes. But what are we to make of people like Frank Rissarro and George Corona, who have learned the ropes and still feel displaced? What are we to make of the children of factory workers who get enough education to start out in a white-collar job, yet feel they are not making enough of themselves, and look back almost wistfully to the craft labor of their parents? All these people know the ropes, and yet feel compelled to keep moving.

This paradox offers a good point at which to assess how much, and how little, we know about the injuries of class. Class society takes away from all the people within it the feeling of secure dignity in the eyes of others and of themselves. It does so in two ways: first, by the images it projects of why people belong to high or low classes—class presented as the ultimate outcome of personal ability; second, by the definition the society makes of the actions to be taken by people of any class to validate their dignity—legitimizations of self which do not, cannot work and so reinforce the original anxiety.

The result of this, we believe, is that the activities which keep people moving in a class society, which make them seek more money, more possessions, higher-status jobs, do not originate in a materialistic desire, or even sensuous appreciation, of things, but out of an attempt to restore a psychological deprivation that the class structure has effected in their lives. In other words, *the psychological motivation instilled by a class society is to heal a doubt about the self rather than create more power over things and other persons in the outer world.*

It might be said that this is an extremely hopeful picture of human motives—that people act to restore themselves rather than to possess and dominate. To which we would reply that no more urgent business in a life can exist than establishing a sense of personal dignity—if forces beyond one's control call the dignity into question from the time one is a schoolchild, it becomes a prior question to power and possession, and indeed a reason why power and possession are sought after at all. Hobbes took as a given the desire of men to dominate, but when attempts to dominate social circumstances—which in the modern world become attempts just to be free of others' power, to be self-sufficient —when these efforts cause such anxiety and uneasiness, how can they be taken as a final, natural desire?

Society, Locke believed, is an agglomeration of individuals. When we know the psychological makeup of a single man, therefore, we know the motivational forces operating in the society as a whole. The uses of injured dignity presented in this chapter, however, cast this formulation, too, in dispute. In consuming for a future time in which they or their children have become whole, men are not trying to keep capitalism alive, nor have they arrived at that identification with the Establishment that Marcuse depicts. What happens, rather, is that manifold acts of personal restoration added one to another, family to family, city to city, become transformed into a force that keeps the wounding society powerful.

Let us contrast the injuries of class in these terms to Max Weber's idea of a Protestant work ethic. Feeling that their worth was uncertain in the eyes of God, Weber wrote, the early Protestants tried to convince each other through acts of self-abnegation that they were worthy of respect; this mentality, Weber believed, was assimilated by the early capitalist entrepreneurs. Although a wrathful God had fled the stage by the time Ben Franklin wrote his aphorisms in Philadelphia, the industrious boy who started with nothing could still believe he made himself worthy of respect, by denying himself present pleasures, in order someday to elevate his social standing.

Weber never intended the Protestant ethic to be equated with the three or four hundred years of industrial capitalism. He intended simply to show how the people who first began to develop surplus capital through savings or other future-oriented activity did so out of a peculiar morality of "earning" respect. The use of this morality has since been to enable entrepreneurs acquiring capital to feel justified in their power; the justification in turn has pushed them to acquire more.

Although the Protestant ethic bears a certain similarity to the hidden dimensions of respect, personal talent, and class we have discussed, it differs in two ways: first, Weber was talking about the justification of economic power among an elite, powerful group of men; second, class morality is now self-defeating, while the Protestant ethic was self-confirming. The ethic provided grounds of moral self-congratulation for people who had to practice delayed material gratification in order to accumulate surplus capital.

The burden of class today is thus a strange phenomenon: social inequality is maintained by creating a morality of anxiety, and this discontent is hard to organize by the Left because the logic of discontent leads people to turn on each other rather than on the "system." The limit on this argument is that the notion of class that has so far appeared in this book is economically primitive, essentially a matter of manual or blue-collar labor as opposed to educated office or professional work. The occupational structure is obviously more complicated than this—indeed, a good criticism of the argument so far made in this book is that it shows the poles of work in the society but nothing about what "class" means emotionally for the great body of workers in between. Then again, class lines are not static, because the forms of work are constantly changing; if manual work is also on the decline in a technological society, then might this analysis of class not be oriented to people who are in fact in a declining, and anxiety-ridden, situation? These are the questions we need to deal with now.

The Census tells us that in 1900, a third of the working population in America were farmers, half were nonrural laborers, both factory and service workers, and only a sixth were engaged in white-collar work. By 1950 farm labor had greatly declined, about half the population remained in manual labor, and white-collar work had greatly increased. This shift is conventionally read as a matter of work becoming more advanced over the half-century, more mental, progressively less physical.*

This gross change would seem to explain why ability is increasingly on people's minds when they analyze their class standing. White-collar, respectable, nonmenial—the terms, as C. Wright Mills has pointed out, have traditionally come from a notion of the greater complexity of "desk" work as opposed to work with the hands. Yet beneath the surface something more puzzling is occurring.

In the last half-century, the Census shows that the greatest growth of white-collar positions has been among such routine tasks as filing, typing, document-processing, and the like. These low-level white-collar jobs, seen usually as "appropriate" for women, now claim the single largest group of workers. During the same period, moreover, there has been a peculiar growth of the professions. If special ability is becoming more important in productive work, one would expect the professions to be expanding and becoming more variegated. Yet the Census shows professions expanding mostly at such supposedly low levels as grade-school teaching; these changes account for almost all of the proportional increase of professional work, and these positions, too, have been filled largely by women. As a contrasting example, the

---

* Figures drawn from an invaluable publication of the Census called *Historical Statistics of the United States*.

percentage of doctors in the work force may actually have declined slightly since 1920.

It becomes, in other words, difficult to explain the increased importance placed on mind when "mind jobs," as Ivar Berg describes them, are not the growth leaders of the work force. The problem is also more complex, because while white-collar labor has grown principally in low-status, routine-skill occupations, manual work has been progressively upgraded since World War I. The percentage of unskilled workers in the work force has steadily declined, while the number of skilled manual workers is rising faster at present than the number of semiskilled workers. Much manual work, furthermore, now involves more elaborate on-the-job education. Apprenticeships and journeymen stints have gradually lengthened and become more demanding.

The increase in low-level white-collar work, jobs which in many cases demand less skill, allow less independence, and offer less pay than skilled manual labor, is partially dissolving the traditional symbolic meaning of "moving up" to the office from the factory. In the nineteenth and early-twentieth centuries the distinction between blue- and white-collar workers made a great deal more sense than it does today. In 1910 an office clerk usually made something like twice as much as an unskilled manual laborer; he tended to have more job security and could look upon his position in relation to the vast majority of workingpeople with an assured sense of doing more skilled and privileged tasks. This has now changed.

Nonetheless, white-collar work still retains an important status difference from manual labor. Jobs like filing, document-processing, and similar bureaucratic tasks are simple, routine, and easily mastered, yet educational requirements for such jobs have become more and more elaborate. In the words of a U.S. Manpower Commission, "a young woman who is hired to type letters is increasingly required to have some college experience before she gets the job, even though the skills required for good job performance could have been mastered when she was barely adolescent." Observers of the growth of purely "technological" industries like the computer field have made the same point: the efficiency in production brought by advances in technology has not eliminated low-level, routine jobs but has rather shifted them around and, in the aggregate, perhaps, even increased them. Yet the assumption of employers is that an increasing amount of education is needed to labor at these simple tasks. It is almost as though mind becomes more important as the uses for mind in new jobs become less.

This paradox applies not just to low-level white-collar work, but increasingly to manual jobs as well. One study of predominantly blue-collar jobs in five industries found little net change in real skill requirements necessary for adequate performance between 1940 and 1965, although there was a considerable rise in the credentials required by employers for these jobs.° (One wonders how much this kind of situation affects the upgrading of manual labor that appears in the Census; but to say this is just to pose the problem in larger terms: why are white-collar and blue-collar work both subject to an escalation of employment credentials that has nothing to do with the substance of work?)

° See Ivar Berg's superb *Education and Jobs: The Great Training Robbery* (New York: Praeger; 1970).

Among blue-collar workers in a textile plant in Mississippi, a study shows that the less-educated workers tend to be more productive, have a lower turnover rate, and fewer absences. Another investigation found this inverse relationship between amount of education and job performance to obtain as well for those in low-skilled white-collar work and even in managerial positions. Ivar Berg, in analyzing such materials, has come to the same conclusion Frank Rissarro did: possession of the qualities of a "good" worker is inversely related to the years of schooling a person has.

And still the rewards of greater income and promotion that are said to flow almost automatically from the exercise of the classic virtues of hard work and diligence are not forthcoming to many manual laborers, because the assumptions of employers generally run contrary to these findings. What they assume is what our culture more generally assumes: mind is productive. Although, as Herbert Gintis points out, most studies have shown liberal arts college courses to have little relationship either to post-college job content or to performance, the degree remains a prime symbol of fitness for work. (Many employers, when queried about this, cite the greater self-assurance, commitment to the organization, and social integration in the organization that they believe better-educated persons to have.)

So strong is this belief in the greater productive power of educated persons that employers tend often to ignore their own measures of productivity and to hire younger, more-educated workers who have quit other employers. As regards salaries, also, the better-educated can expect a discounting of their past performance elsewhere, and a salary rate established instead on the basis of their degrees.

In large corporations, this management practice of moving more-educated people from the outside into the higher-skilled positions puts a ceiling on the possibilities for promotion for less-educated workers. The promotional rewards open to these workers are limited largely to becoming foremen or moving into low-level white-collar positions. Thus, less-educated people achieve through steady hard work at one job lesser rewards than those open to less-stable, better-educated workers because of their academic credentials.

Why are these seemingly illogical changes taking place? In our view, this gap between productivity and certified knowledge exists because it permits class lines to be maintained as the job categories that define particular classes change. By this, we mean that the sheer inequality of classes can be maintained even as the productive "infrastructure" evolves into a new form.

Consider what the gap between productivity and certified knowledge means in terms of the evolution of new patterns of work: first, the productive order is creating a new mass of people who do routine tasks—i.e., whose freedom of choice on the job is extremely limited. Second, this mass of white-collar workers is enmeshed in a set of self-contradictory status symbols. The bulk of the recruits into expanded white-collar jobs are young people most of whose parents, according to such analysts as Blau and Duncan, were blue-collar workers. Those parents, working in the 1950's and '60's, were the first generation of manual laborers to pass in significant numbers from a life of scarcity and constant economic insecurity to a life of some affluence. Crossing the line was presented to them as, and indeed they hoped it would mean, a qualitative change in their lives—

more freedom, a chance to arrange their lives so that they could command the respect of people outside the ethnic villages. Crossing the barrier, however, has not in fact yielded the promised emotional gratifications, as we have tried to show. And, among the sons and daughters, crossing the barrier into white-collar work has produced the same emotional frustration.

To get a white-collar job you must stay in school. Schooling is supposed to develop your internal powers, make you as a person more powerful in relation to the productive order of the society; the move into white-collar work is in this way a consequence of your having become a more developed human being. Yet most of those flowing into white-collar work find the reality quite different—the content of the work in fact requires very little mind at all. How is someone who feels dissatisfied selling shoes or stamping papers to make sense of what is happening in comparing his or her "better" job to the hard physical labor of his or her father? What does it mean to such a young person that he or she has stayed in school, a good child, only to feel, as Donald Warren puts it, that in crossing the line you have to start again at the bottom?

As we saw in Chapter 2, these questions are answered by the people caught up in this historical shift as a problem of their own personalities, as a problem of their inadequate ability to cope. The utility of that feeling is what we are now in a position to understand: although certification of mind for these low-level white-collar jobs has little to do with job performance, it serves a purpose in creating certain moral symbols around work. These symbols will induce people, on logical and rational grounds, to feel that their membership in the new mass is just as much a personal responsibility, and as tinged with overtones of questioned personal adequacy, as was their parents' membership in the old working class. The certification of mind through formal education is, then, a necessity to keep class inequality alive in a changing set of productive relations. Even more important, by making people feel a disparity between what they ought to be as persons as a result of being educated and what they experience directly in their new work, such certification persuades them that the onus rests on themselves.

For the older generation of manual laborers, the result of bearing the burden of this responsibility is not despair, but a resolve to exert a peculiar discipline, the discipline of self-sacrifice, in order to make the future better. For the young from such families who are filling up the new white-collar jobs, that personal resolution is similarly carried on. After our first interviews with mobile people, we were puzzled by what we had heard; if people felt life was a rat race, and they had enough to get by, why keep running? What we learned to hear was an assumption behind the complaints of getting nowhere: if a person feels as though *he* is running—even if he has been made to run—and he fails to win, to quit racing is humiliating. The result of the conflict between the status and the content of white-collar work is that people like George Corona feel even more future-oriented than before: it's just up to now that they aren't making the most of their new position in society. Inadequacy in this situation serves as a spur to self-discipline rather than revolt.

Let us state this in a general form: Calling people's dignity into question is a means by which a class society can create new classes of limited freedom as the old classes disappear. The change of class is portrayed in the society as a matter of improvement, of success, of upward mobility; the frustration and resentment threatened by the gap between promised reward and continued constraint of freedom is diverted into a problem of the self, so that even as the young shoe salesman quoted two chapters back feels angry about what has happened in his life, his anger at the "system" is undercut because inwardly he also blames himself for not making something of his opportunities. We are back to the idea of *legitimization* posed in discussing the Watson School, only now it is a matter of the legitimization of an ongoing limitation on freedom, under the surface of a change in the economic character of the class structure.

But just as the schoolchildren were not entirely the pawns of the figures of authority in the school, adults are not passive victims in this scheme. The people we interviewed in Boston had very definite ideas about what justice was in the society, in particular what justice meant in terms of equality of opportunity to change classes.

Interestingly, the views we heard expressed by white ethnic workers about the nature of equal opportunity are quite similar to what other researchers report as the attitudes of black workers. Equal opportunity is not just a chance to compete with others on an equal starting line, it represents a chance to change your personality.

"Like if someone isn't roped in, he can find out what's best for him," says a black mechanic. "You give a man a chance to start off in life the same as everyone, he can find out what he wants, what he can do," says a white tailor. Similarly, in the late eighteenth century "careers open to talent" meant to the lower bourgeoisie something different from just a chance to get rich. If careers became open to talent, then they could create in themselves the same inner richness of feeling and culture higher-born people had.

Equality of opportunity would make everyone responsible for his social position. The tailor, for instance, later remarked, "If everyone gets a fair break, then what happens to him is his business . . . if things don't work out, that's his problem." During the height of the entrepreneurial era in America in the 1870's, the Horatio Alger stories made a constant plea for equal opportunity, but as insistently proclaimed that once a man had the opportunity to do what he wanted, once, that is, he was ready to act, his success or failure was entirely a personal problem. Society then somehow disappeared from the scene, and his fate was a matter of personal strength and character.

Whenever we had a chance in Boston to talk about the idea of opportunity, we felt engaged on two levels of discourse. On the surface, there would be a declaration from a person that if he had had the advantages middle-class people enjoy, he would have been able to make what he wanted of his life. This was an affirmation among these men that they could be just as strong, just as free, as anyone else if they had the chance. There would, however, be something hidden below this surface feeling. These were, after all, people who had experienced frustration, who had suffered from a gnawing sense of powerlessness, who had been treated for most of their lives as undistinctive. All of that experience, which had to do with the structure of class, had presented itself to them as a problem in the structure of their own characters; and so there lay an unspoken distrust of themselves below the surface, a feeling of doubt. When in a family a person crosses the barrier, gets a better job and thus the chance to make something of himself, the cultural environment reinforces the problem in the work structure itself: past adds to present the fear he will not be good enough to develop himself.

The possibility of failure is the most uncomfortable phenomenon in American life. There is no room for failure in our schemes of respect, unless the failure is found to result from some cataclysmic event like the Great Depression. There is, as well, indifference to those who do not move ahead. Failures and static people—the nobodies Sammy Glick so feared—are seen as having undeveloped personalities; the uncomfortable feelings about those who do not "make something of themselves" when they have a chance, come out of an assumption that men can be respected only as they become in some way distinctive, as they stand out from the mass.

Equality of opportunity is not, therefore, an ideal framed to encourage men who are frustrated, defeated, or unsure of themselves. It is at best a message that, were society fair, they would have a chance to escape being "nobodies."

Thus does the justice of "equal opportunity" slide back to a dilemma of personal worth. When an opportunity like more education or a better job opens up that will erase some disability felt before, society seems suddenly to make itself invisible, leaving the individual to grapple with class change as though his personal strength must suffice for all he faces.

In recent years, writers like Serge Mallet have sought to describe the evolution of a "new working class" along different lines. Mallet has seized on an idea contained in Alain Touraine's theory of a post-industrial society. Class as we know it, Touraine believes, is disappearing because the source of production, the energy to make the economic machine go, has shifted from capital to mind, from the banks to the laboratory and classroom. Perhaps that is so, Mallet observes, but then in the laboratory and classroom a new class of oppressed workers has grown up, deprived of the fruits of their labor as surely as the steelworkers in the factories financed by the banks were so deprived. A worker-student alliance is possible, Mallet and André Gorz believe, because students and technicians in the education-research complex are now in the same position as workers have always been.

These are sensible ideas, but they assume that mind is now being used for production, that thought is being appropriated by the modern capitalist state for new techniques, goods, and services as directly as the physical effort of thousands of coal workers was once appropriated so that British industrial magnates could have their floating gondola parties at the Savoy.

The situation we have described, by contrast, is one in which certificates of mind and intellectual development have no use once the shoe salesman or office worker hits the job; two years of "liberal arts" is a rite of passage with no innate productive function—save, perhaps, to keep the young off the job market. The use of this barrier, in the debased utilitarianism we see, is to create the kind of conflict between expectation and reality that makes the shoe salesman or office worker feel he isn't making use of his opportunities, that he has to keep trying because he isn't getting anywhere. The use of this conflict is for discipline, not theft.

Several years ago, before it fell on evil days, Students for a Democratic Society had a study group concerned with the "new working class" of shoe salesmen, secretaries, and office clerks. In 1964 Richard Sennett attended some open sessions held in Chicago about the new working class conceived in these terms; for him, the changes are striking between how the matter was conceived by the group then, from the outside, and how it looks to him now, having talked at length with people who have passed into this new class from blue-collar homes.

Then, the matter seemed all about physical oppression: the work of secretaries, file clerks, and other office workers is exhausting, the physical routine is unrelieved, the pay is terrible, and so on; the office is an unregenerate factory, without even the elementary safeguards unions can enforce.

Now, those charges still seem true but to miss the point. A person can put up with a great deal of physical privation if he believes what he is doing is worthwhile. In one frame of reference, white-collar workers from blue-collar families do believe their work is worthwhile; wearing a suit and tie, going downtown to the office—these things command a certain prestige among peers and parents. But the emotional level at which self-respect becomes entangled with the class system is much deeper than this. One is twenty-one, with all sorts of dreams of opportunity, others look to one as a person who is going to make something of himself, and one feels frustrated pushing papers as a clerk, or bored selling shoes. That is where the real oppression of the new working class begins, for everything in the society prompts a kid to feel his insides are therefore messed up. Perhaps the most devilish part of the utility of injuring dignity on these grounds is that the kid has probably had a year or two of college to qualify him for the office. If education is a tool for making him free, if he has come through that rite of passage which is supposed to "develop" him, no matter how much he *knows* "the system" is rotten, he has to fight a doubt about himself first to be able unreservedly to fight the world.

We stress this matter so much because this hidden continuity in the language of class points to a sense of mass bitterness and frustration we believe will keep growing, even if all taxes on workers are abolished, racial conflicts eliminated, and wars no longer drain off the sons of workers and the poor.

Everything in the family lives of the workers we spoke to is oriented to moving the child over a barrier. A typical comment: "My child must be educated. I don't want to push him, but that's the only way he can do what he wants." One family went so far as to migrate from a predominantly Italian immigrant community where both parents were born and all their family and friends live, to a predominantly Jewish, lower-middle-class suburb where they don't know anyone but where the "Jewish schools" are reputed to be much better. Most parents, however, view the right attitudes towards schooling as perhaps more important than the schools themselves. "Give James or Cathy the right ideas about school and they'll make the most of themselves almost anywhere," said one parent. It is not that the quality of the schools is unimportant, but that a parent feels primary responsibility for his child's right attitude to rest upon himself.

That responsibility has a special and pathetic cast. "If you don't have them degrees, they're gonna treat you like you was nothing," says a garbage collector to his children. "I say to Sheila," remarks an electrician, "you do that homework, or you'll wind up in the same boat like me . . . It's for your own good you got to study."

Education, as we have seen, will not simply make their children different; it will be set against a character failing the parents see in their own youth. "I was just stupid, I didn't care," said a longshoreman. "But my kids is going to be different." "If I hadn't quit school to make a fast buck, I wouldn't be where I am today," said another man.

If we read changes in job structure right, however, these parental longings are going to be increasingly frustrated in coming years. Lifetimes of parental dedication are going to seem to come to no good end, not for the parents perhaps as much as for the young themselves. For the young of the working class, as John Gagnon has said, have a tremendous "burden of hope" placed on them, a hope circumstances beyond their control may well defeat. Interviewers of youth from working-class homes* have found a malaise among these kids greater though more inarticulate than the discontent of the glamour children of the 1960's. Where will it lead? The only use we can envision for destructive replacement is as an incentive for discipline, for inspiring the future-oriented resolve to "make something of oneself." Perhaps, however, the hidden system of class is not strong enough to maintain this function. We have spoken of the utility of injured dignity, but what is useful and order-maintaining is not necessarily permanent. The creation of a new mass may meet intangible resistance the more these kids "lose faith"—a phrase that cuts both ways: a boy like James

---

* The work of Gagnon and John Simon in Chicago is perhaps the most thorough in this field.

feels he has inadequately used his opportunities to make something of himself, and at the same time he has ceased to believe he could.

Lévi-Strauss has remarked that the mask images of a god can be changed only so many times in a tribe before men cease to believe that God can ever be depicted on a mask. Perhaps, in the same way, the symbols of dignity—possessions, better jobs—can be replaced only so many times before the idea that dignity can be conveyed in such a symbolic transaction may be destroyed. In this, we may be putting too much of a "burden of hope" on the kids; but a belief in the American Dream seems exhausted in their lives—or will things change when they grow up, and have families of their own to sacrifice for?

American capitalism has set up a terrible test of itself. It imposes a certain obligation on men to develop themselves, yet to maintain itself the economic structure must continually replace the symbols of what development is. Affluence orients men to an unknown future, yet that sense of future time, too, is destructive; the child growing differently leaves the parent no common ground to share with him. If for economic reasons society must destroy as soon as it creates, how long will men believe that an unremitting effort to validate themselves will bring an eventual reign of respect?

PART TWO

DREAMS AND
DEFENSES

CHAPTER IV

THE DIVIDED
SELF

The puzzles of freedom and dignity described so far ought
to drive people mad. Dignity is as compelling a human need
as food or sex, and yet here is a society which casts the mass
of its people into limbo, never satisfying their hunger for
dignity, nor yet so explicitly depriving them that the task of
proving dignity seems an unreasonable burden, and revolt
against the society the only reasonable alternative. However, most of the people who appear in the pages of this
book are not on the edge of nervous collapse, nor at that
point of despair where revolt is kindled. On the contrary,
they get by from day to day with a sense of balance, with a
certain distance from the problems of class and class consciousness.

The capacity of a human being to protect himself from
society, to live a life as more than a creature of circumstance, is a psychological strength that is often described as
"innate" to the psyche. That is, the distance people put between themselves and their social problems is explained by
writers like Wilhelm Dilthey as the strength people have to

escape into themselves, to shut society out. This seems perfectly logical, and yet it is too simple: if society is powerful enough to wound people at a very deep emotional level— which is where the wounds inflicted on dignity are—the power to shut society out would have to be a transcendental, almost miraculous one.

People never lose consciousness *of* society. What human consciousness can do is create new patterns out of the information society feeds to it, patterns which deaden or distance the emotional impact of the information. The more the effects of information from a hostile or repressive society are neutralized through these special patterns, the more balance and sanity human beings achieve. Throughout this book, we have treated personal consciousness as something other than a storage locker or receptacle for social information; consciousness, we think, is an active human power. What we would now like to do is show concretely how it acts to defend the human being from society by rearranging the information society furnishes about the nature of human dignity. We hope to show how this defense is more complicated than simply "shutting out" a bad society, more than an escape through willfully ignoring what is happening outside the self. We want to show how this defense works—and how successful it is—by looking at a peculiar kind of alienation.

"Join power and love," Nietzsche once wrote, "then you can never be hurt." It is an extraordinary doctrine: it says man knows no real love until he possesses power, it says love without power is always subject to violation, to betrayal, to contempt. There is, Nietzsche wrote, no pure love.

But what if you feel powerless? How *can* you then join love to power?

These questions persistently appear reflected in the emotional injuries of class: in the conflict between fraternity and individual ability, in the sacrificial attempts to make power out of one's love. The attempt to join the two realms seems only to increase the feeling of powerlessness.

Should love and power, then, be kept apart?

If love and power are kept apart, if love is kept pure in order that men transcend their circumstances, men alienate themselves. The word "alienate" has as one of its roots (*alienatus, alienare*) the sense of making two realms foreign to each other, to make them strangers. To speak of estranging love and power, is to talk of men alienating two spheres of being within themselves, willfully making strange these two forms of experience, rather than being alienated by external forces. Is the practice of alienation, then, a way of defending oneself? The question asks really whether a phenomenon long regarded as a sign of cultural sickness might not in fact be an assertion of sanity.

"They gave me a pay raise when the south wall mess was straightened out," says a young plumber to explain a feat of re-engineering he did on a construction project with faulty plans. Although obviously quite pleased with what he had done, the plumber could not use "I did" to describe what in fact he did do; instead, "the south wall mess was straightened out." Similarly, George Corona "was moved" from supervising two men to nine; William O'Malley "was put to work" on the most intricate machine on the line; Frank Rissarro, ill-educated, has been "lucky enough" to hold a demanding white-collar job for several years. In each case the passive voice replaces an "I," an I that would otherwise seem the master of a situation.

The use of the passive voice in these situations simply reflects outer reality in one respect: even though it is the worker who is acting, he does so under the control of some-one else. The "mess" the plumber faced was made by an-other; the rewards the others received were given them by an employer.

The use of the passive voice, however, does something more than define responsibility. Recall that Rissarro talked of his successes as things he gained through imposture, or because others did not know who he "really" was. His wife, he says, would not have married him if she had known he was uneducated and came from a "poor background." When a listener hears Rissarro say such things, the listener's first thought is that he is deluding himself: his speech and mannerisms are all of the ethnic ghetto, so how could he think he would ever "fool" anyone about himself?

The answer is that as long as he is fooling them, as long as he feels himself to be an impostor, the real person within him is not compromised by trying to win respect. The man who likes working with his hands, the father who enjoys his children, is a different person from ambitious Frank, the pa-terfamilias who demands that his kids obey him.

Rissarro's consciousness becomes an actor, an arranger of the social world, by putting into one compartment those ex-ercises of personal power that make a man stand out, earn material rewards and the emotional reward of new respect, and into another compartment the real self. He alienates the active, performing self, seeking recognition from others as a distinctive individual, from the passive self that just wants to be, to enjoy family and friends, to love them.

Here is how a young man describes a community clean-up project in which he won an award: "We really did a good job . . . There was twelve of us, and each went over four blocks, picking up broken bottles and trash and the like . . . We received that civic award, you know, from Kiwanis . . ." The interviewer asks about a scholarship this young man later received from the same group as a result of this work: "Um . . . they gave out these scholarships, they gave one to me . . ."

The interviewer asks, "Was it because of the community work you did?" and he replies, "Yeah, the community work that was done there, they probably were influenced by that." Again the shift from active to passive, the person disappears when the individual stands out. It is almost as though two times of living coexist at once, as in this woman's recollection of her graduation:

"I remember my own high school graduation so clearly. I was wearing a white dress and we sat in chairs on the stage . . . they had us sit in those chairs because they were giving awards to students who had done well in school . . . yes, they were giving the awards to them and the students were embarrassed, you know, in front of everybody."

"Were you one of those students?"

"Yes . . . I remember looking at my boyfriend out in the audience, he had a suit on and it looked so strange, like every seam would burst . . . the audience looking up on those people on the stage, and then the procession, such beautiful music and all, and they had those people on the stage go first, and then the audience . . ."

"Were you embarrassed by going first?"

"Oh, it was a lovely affair, I didn't mind."

Mary is there on stage, and yet the honor of being there is something happening to her.

The loss of "I" defends a person from two threats. First of all, it wards off social isolation. If I act as though my "real" self is someone divorced from the person who does well in situations when higher authority asks it, if my competence or power to cope is held at arm's length, as though it were a power external to me as a human being, then when I achieve a new position or other reward from a higher power, I can pass it off as something *I* didn't do.

Advancement through approval, promotion, even such mundane cues as having a superior ask one's opinion or advice, now do not have to get in the way of fraternity with those around me who have not changed. I can still be accepted as a friend, as someone who is not deserting them or putting them in a bad light, because "I" really have not done anything to make this change occur. Passivity has a real place in the life of men who want friends, because the institutions in which men pass their days make it so.

This language of self also deals with the threat of being accepted as an individual—in the sense of a special person, passivity shields the person from a wound contained in a seemingly flattering state.

Protective alienation of the real person from the performing individual appears strikingly in the life of a middle-aged asbestos worker. A few years after the early death of his first wife, he married a woman who once was convicted for prostitution. His relatives think he has demeaned himself by marrying the "slut," as they call her. They are hysterical on this subject, and he defends himself by never showing his reactions to what they are saying, reactions of intense disgust and loathing; instead he maintains, by an iron will, a rational posture toward them, and evades all show of emotion in explaining and defending himself.

On the surface, such behavior would seem to involve a split in which the loving person within the self stays passive. But in fact, this is a different kind of defensive phenomenon: the man doesn't want the respect of his relatives. He feels that he is exerting his power as a man when he keeps silent in the face of this taunting; he is protecting his relationship with his wife. Love and power are joined in this silence—the silence is not a passive disconnection.

In situations where he has to perform for authority, and has been praised, an alienated passivity does arise. In four years of Navy service, he compiled an outstanding record, was promoted several times, and once decorated for a courageous act which saved a ship's heating system from exploding. He is proud of these awards, yet he treats them offhandedly. Keeping honors at arm's length is especially important for the preservation of fraternity in the military; as Morris Janowitz has noted, once a man at mess betrays any pleasure at the promotions or decorations he has received, his chances of eating alone in the future are dramatically increased. But there is another consideration: the more a person becomes emotionally involved in rewards from higher authority, the more *dependent* he becomes on someone else who is not a comrade for the things that give him self-respect. "You ask me about how *I* felt about the Navy? Jesus, I don't know . . . I mean, I got through it, right? I kept my nose clean, I didn't get involved, I didn't let nothing go to my head . . . You 'go Navy,' like in the ads, shit, there's nothing left of you!"

The divorce of the real person from the institution's individual is a way to ward off becoming an "institutional man." In studies of tasks at work, such as Blauner's *Alienation and Freedom*, alienation appears as a matter of losing any sense

197

of individuality or personal creativity in performing a task. Blauner speaks, for example, of the difference between tasks in which a man can set his own pace, stopping for a cup of coffee if he wants, and tasks where, Chaplinesque, he conforms to a strict time schedule, feeling alienated by the work. But in situations where a man like this asbestos worker alienates, where he makes his person foreign to his performance, it is approval from authority rather than the task that is at issue.

In the last chapter, we looked at how an employer, faced with many employees who are equally qualified, must promote on the basis of intuition; he mystifies the employee by appearing to know about the subordinate what the subordinate does not know about himself. Intuitive feeling becomes subject to perversion, so that someone or something above the employee has the means to direct his life in ways beyond his power to understand.

What is the individual to do in response? To maintain the meaning of "you" feeling, "you" caring, "you" in control of yourself, "you" must then ward off any emotional identification with the hierarchy. "You" has to be a dimension of the self that lies low when performing. The response of the asbestos worker in the Navy, the woman graduating, the plumber promoted, when hierarchies threaten bonds of friendship, is thus reinforced by a fear of losing the mark of humanity—intuition and the capacity to feel.

This may seem like reading too much into situations where people are just going about their business at work. Yet when the worlds of love and performance did touch, in a variety of incidents related to us, the effect was depressing in a way the notion of business-as-usual doesn't explain.

A good example is offered by two instances where workers, caught in that great con game of being sold expensive encyclopedias so little Johnny won't be educationally deprived, resolved to do a few months overtime to pay the hundreds of dollars the books cost.

"There was nothing to it, people do it all the time. I mean, when I sat down calmly and thought about it, what the hell, it was just three months . . . but I felt like shit the whole time, very depressed even . . . you know, if I worked the regular day shift everything was all right, and the moment I hit the overtime, I felt terrible."

The twelve years this man has spent as a laborer has accustomed him to think of work as a place where there is no room for the family man who loves his wife and child. The two worlds, consciously, are separate. And within the workplace, in exactly the same way, this man who holds the line so that an arthritic co-worker doesn't fall behind, feels also divorced from the employee who looks good to the foreman. Yet to pay for those encyclopedias, he now has consciously to cross these lines. His care for his child at home makes him temporarily look at his work as directly connected to a loving act; the world of loving and the world of competence temporarily fuse.

What is the result? Not some new meaning and gratification in his work, but a sense of depression and unhappiness. For when he has to act as though power and love were on a continuum in his life, he becomes afraid that love will be violated—almost, as it were, dragged down into the mud—by being placed on a level with the acts of work competence he performs for others. Here is how he puts it: "Yeah, very depressing. I can't figure it out . . . So many hours a book, right? . . . it's simple . . . but then I, to tell you the truth, *like I started resenting the kid for putting me through this* . . . I can't really explain it—but like it's—*things were touching that shouldn't touch* . . . and I know it's not just me, lots of guys sometimes can't stand the overtime."

Here is another man: "Don't you see what I mean, it's like for the family you shouldn't have to be the one who brings in the money, you know, just that . . . you got to be more, I mean, I know who I am—more than just the bank account, you know?"

These men are not worried about sacrifice as such: sacrifice works when a man establishes a balance, a feeling of a protected inner self that co-exists with, and loves more openly, than the sacrificer whose acts of love are also acts of power. Each of the people who think of themselves as sacrificing for their families draws a unique boundary line for himself between the acts that *demonstrate* their affection for the family, and acts that express the affection itself. Whereas for the two men quoted above, being away from home on overtime violates that boundary, for Bertin it does not. For a woman married to a streetsweeper, taking care of her young grandchild so that her daughter could go out to work was a demonstration of affection, although a sacrifice of her own time, but taking care of her own mother, too poor to enter an old-age home, was resented as an "intrusion on my life." In other words, people whose material freedom or freedom to act in an institutional setting is limited in a threatening way, make freedom for themselves by constructing reality so that the real part of themselves must feel free of performing *in response to* the demands of another—it is in this sense that we have linked the idea of spontaneity to this real self which appears to the outer world as passive.

The face of this real self to the institutional world, the passive voice and tone, has been picked up by hostile commentators on workers, in particular, as a proof that workers "get what they deserve." The charge cites workers' supposed obsession with the immediate events of everyday life, their slavery to routines and fear of change of new jobs or tasks, even though workers might "get somewhere" by doing them; conservative studies cite all sorts of missed opportunities in large organizations, chances for change or advancement workers fail to take.

Sacrifice, as we have seen, makes men future-oriented. They are not "stuck" in the present; indeed, the poorer the families we spoke to, the more they framed the goodness of life for themselves in terms of a life they had yet to lead. What is at issue is the fact that the transition to that better future is inscrutable. Men know they are supposed to work hard, and do the best they can. They see that a few do "make it," but not, as far as can be seen, because of anything different about them. To keep going in the face of this riddle, a defense, which may appear to the outsider as fatalism, is needed.

R. D. Laing has spoken of an "ontological security" he feels human beings have to achieve, a feeling that the self can survive whatever it encounters in the world. A person who is "ontologically secure" is open to new, disruptive, even painful experience; he has achieved the strength to become vulnerable. Perhaps it is because, as sociologists, we look at people from the outside in, rather than the inside out, that this idea seems to us to miss something. Society imposes the necessity for defensiveness: in a hierarchical organization, to leave yourself open to the new experience the organization offers is to risk being wiped out or lost. Only a blind man, or someone who did indeed have "false consciousness" of his own strength in relation to the organization, would take the risk. But getting from day to day is at least something one can trust. It is this self-protective frame of mind that often appears on the surface of a life like Carl Dorian's as a lack of enterprise.

What happens when the organization deals a different hand, when it singles out an individual for clear-cut failure? If a worker feels dissociated from his work when he is successful at it, surely when he is laid off or fired, the dissociation should be even greater. To keep from getting hurt, he should try to put even more distance between the real person and the individual.

For the two months before we talked to him, the asbestos worker was laid off. It was a strain financially, but fortunately he had enough in the bank to see himself and his family through most of the period. Since he had been so stoical in the face of great provocation from his relatives, one would expect him to react the same way to this economic crisis he had recently passed through. But in the interview he got very upset and distraught over having been denied a job by economic forces outside his control; he felt, he said, as if there were "nothing left" of him when he was laid off. Further, although he felt betrayed by his employer, a small-time contractor, he worried about whether the contractor had ever really approved of his work.

The important element here is his worry about what his boss really must have thought about him. Did your boss like your work? he was asked. "Yah, very much, but see—when he had to—when I lost the job, he was kind of distant. Not mean, I knew he was hurting financially, but like he wouldn't let me talk to him about it . . . yeah, very distant, you might say, sort of avoiding me . . ."

In looking at the notions of ability in the early I.Q. tests, we saw that people who did more poorly than the mass also stood out as special individuals on the bell-shaped curve. Leaving aside the scientific shakiness of that finding, let us transfer the metaphor: people who are explicitly rejected or penalized economically in the society also stand out as individuals.

When the asbestos worker says that for the previous two months he had felt very much alone; when Frank Rissarro says that at the point of being put in a special class for problem kids, no one seemed to care about him; when, after he had once been laid off, the pipe fitter next door to the schoolteacher Mr. Arnold had "this crazy thought that people were avoiding me," they are all really saying that splitting the fraternal, caring self from one's competence doesn't work as a defense against failure. It is a defense against approval, against which no man would seem to have to defend himself. In failing, however, *all* of a person does so—and it makes him feel alone.

When a person is individualized by special rejection, however, he too feels something mystifying about the power judging him. The asbestos worker cannot fathom what his boss thinks about him, nor could Rissarro understand why he was put into the special class. Indeed, many metaphors of rejection have this Job-like quality: the images of punishment Melanie Klein describes as held by small children

share with those held by the dismissed worker that same element of puzzlement as to why authority acts as it does.

We have spoken mostly in this book of power as a human
experience for those who are on the receiving end of it. But
the Watson School teachers and George Corona also have
problems with the power they wield, problems of ambivalence and self-doubt that parallel those of their charges. In
the act of singling someone out for individual disapproval, a
power figure, too, must defend himself; in this situation, he
has need of the same kinds of defenses a subordinate needs
when he or she is approved. Here is a shop foreman reflecting on the demotion of one of his men, with whom he had
once been friendly: "God, I felt like shit about it . . . then
things got a little tense between me and Bert, you might
say—I mean, it wasn't really my decision and he knew it
. . . but what happened after a few months—well, it just
got easier not to be friends . . . like the only way he could
believe it wasn't my fault was if we were just—um—just
sort of working together, so that there wasn't any friendship,
wasn't anything personal between us . . . for me I guess it
was the same—when there wasn't anything personal between us any more, I didn't feel so bad about his hard luck."

For the superior, it is an altogether normal reaction. If I,
who am higher, stop interacting personally and emotionally
with people who are lower, the guilt and uneasiness about
being in a higher position, and causing someone pain, can be
stilled. What Bruno Bettelheim calls the "guilt of surviving"
is in a transmuted way engaged here. For the superior, like
the shop foreman who delivers an explicit rejection, to act
as though the human self, the real self, is not on the job, to
act as though personally he is not enmeshed or identified

with this power situation in which he deals out pain—this serves to avoid a whole range of troubling and irresolvable conflicts about his responsibility. Since the foreman or the contractor does not control the economy, his feeling that he must not allow his humanity to be engaged is perfectly rational; *he* cannot solve the riddle of his own survival when others suffer.

"I guess I was lucky, though I worked damn hard for the good things in my life," says an assistant school principal, "but I'll tell you this, you got to deal with the kids in this school without thinking too much about the past—otherwise I couldn't be good at my job, you know . . . I'll tell you something, life is too mixed up for any school principal once he goes soft. They say this is a strict school; that's true, and the reason is that once you start bending and getting permissive, no matter who you are, no matter if you're like me and it breaks your heart to see so many of these kids come to nothing, because I know that life . . . you have to protect yourself by being fair and impartial and avoiding—permissiveness."

"Permissiveness" is a code word. It means here the fear of losing your sense of authority through compassion, through being touched by the plight of others. It means chaos and a loss of authority coming, not out of the rebellion of children, but the humanity of adults. That is one reason why this assistant principal holds himself back, does not engage the whole, feeling man he is on the job. The rules of survivorship under authority mean he can do no other without losing his job; he has made himself cold and impersonal in school in order to retain a sense of his own integrity.

The result, however, when misfortune strikes those

below, is that just when they need reassurance most, the defenses their superiors erect to protect their own feelings permit sharing and human warmth the least. The foreman cannot tell Bert he feels sorry for him when the demotion comes because this would make him feel too bad about himself; the asbestos worker's boss acts distant and untouchable, for otherwise he would feel responsible for the pain he is causing this man—and he cannot be responsible, because he did not cause the recession. The irony created by the compassion of men in power who feel guilty is that all of a worker is wiped out by this separation of love and power during misfortune. The secret selves of employer and employee do not touch.

IS THIS DEFENSE SCHIZOPHRENIC?

The split of the real person and the performing individual seemed to us at first very close to the kind of divided selfhood psychiatrists call schizophrenia. In the wake of such books as Laing's *The Politics of Experience*, it has become common to talk about schizophrenic social structures that account for divisions of self over the whole of the society, not just among the few on whom the label "schizophrenic" is pinned. And, given the class dynamics of praising, of selection and social division, the matter in such terms seems quite sensible: the rules of selection do not let all men have "distinctive character," and the human response to that unfairness is for the affected individuals to split up character itself.

But there are problems with this approach, first of all because, while it appears to add a new dimension, it in fact washes over important social differences. A person conventionally labeled insane may just be more sensitive to the contradictions of the social order, but what then makes the multitude walking around in a state of "sanity" insensitive? Are they all insensitive in the same way?

Divisions of the self are treated today as related to definitions of sanity, but these divisions have much richer historical dimensions. Religious conversion, in most of the Protestant sects, results from an experience of divided self, where the sinner suddenly finds born within him urges that seem to have nothing to do with worldly feelings, so that he comes to exist in two different frames of reference. For centuries that division of the self was regarded as an ennobling occurrence in a man's life. In autobiographies of nineteenth-century radicals like Alexander Herzen, the process of political conversion involves the same kind of division of self: a man gets along according to the lights of a world he abhors, and carries within himself a vision of a world he does not yet know which also guides his actions. Indeed, unless we are to say that all moral dreaming touches on the line between sanity and insanity, these splits in the self have to be taken out of an exclusively psychiatric context.

The specific way in which the person is divided from the individual differs from the splits in self which touch on the issue of sanity. The early works of Laing, such as *The Divided Self* and *Sanity, Madness and the Family* (written with A. Esterson), poignantly convey the inner feelings and the disconnected language of a human being pulled apart. The act of dividing the self creates terrible pain and suffering—there is nothing calming about it. By contrast, in the life of a manual worker who acts as though his work situation or acceptance by his superiors has nothing to do with his real self, the inner division *is* calming. The arrangement of consciousness which puts competence "out there" gives a person boundaries within which he can feel freely and without a sense of responsibility for his social position. Dividing the self defends against the pain a person would otherwise feel, if he had to submit the whole of himself to a society which makes his position a vulnerable and anxiety-laden one. In this sense, dividing the self in terms of real me and performing me has little to do with the agony that is involved in schizophrenic experience.

There is a question of structure involved as well. The popular notion of a schizophrenic used to be of a person who led a double life, who was literally two-selved, along the lines of Jekyll and Hyde. This is actually a rare phenomenon medically. A more precise meaning of schizophrenia has been formed by Gregory Bateson and his colleagues, who have made intensive studies of the language schizophrenics use to describe what they feel. Bateson came to the conclusion that the sense of a divided self, or of contradictory modes of self, occurs in the life of a schizophrenic because he is caught in what Bateson calls "a double bind."

A double bind is a set of mutually contradictory commands which an individual tries to obey, in situations where he cannot "leave the field" of commands. If my father tells me to do my chores and then gets angry when I do them because I have not done my homework, I am caught in a double bind. I cannot "leave the field" of commands because the love of my parent is made to depend on whether I am a dutiful child, and I need his love. What then am I to do?

This becomes a schizophrenic situation, in Bateson's scheme, when I try to obey both commands at once, making dishwashing motions while reading, or calling garden tools by the names of famous poets in my literature textbook. Bateson explains such contradictory or disconnected behavior in the daily lives of schizophrenic patients in terms of their having perceived contradictory commands for earning love.

At first glance, the double bind concept might indeed seem to fit the relationship to authority described here. Being competent and so earning acceptance from above means a person risks losing acceptance from those around him. But there is a difference. The commands that the children get in Watson School, that Carl Dorian, William O'Malley, or Frank Rissarro get at work, are straightforward: do what I tell you the best you can. What I am asking does not itself involve any contradiction—I want you to solve this problem, or build a shelf, or sweep the floor. The contradiction is introduced by the person who is taking orders; *he* makes the situation more complex by measuring that command–reward relationship against his own feelings of fraternity and sensitivity to others.

Because human beings are not hapless victims following blindly a game of behavioristic chess, because consciousness is an active process arranging social information, people feel threatened. The person sees beyond the institutional demands, puts the institutional obligations against a set of humane values, and that is what makes the problem for him. Whereas a double bind expresses an impossibility confronting the human being—you must work and you must not work—a person who responds to the simple and real command, Work! prove yourself! by feeling, I'll do the work but *I* won't be there doing it, has himself introduced a contradiction in the face of orders and class lines; and he or she then alienates him- or herself to ward off the pain that the contradiction threatens to cause.

Class is not, in other words, a system that forces people to become schizophrenic. These divides in self are rather a response that occurs because men are greater than the system they live under.

If a psychiatric approach misses what happens when people feel something essentially "them" is absent in being competent, however, is there something uniquely "working class" about this phenomenon?

VARIETIES OF SELF-DEFENSE

Some interesting interviews have been done at various colleges with strongly motivated "high-achieving" students with no obvious psychiatric disorders. These students from MIT, the University of Chicago, and Harvard all spoke of their work in school and their standing in the eyes of their teachers as only a part of themselves, and not really the sphere of activity where they felt they acted "naturally." In some of the Harvard interviews, when the investigator pressed the students further, he got reactions involving what he called a division between inauthenticity and authenticity. Authenticity was a state of feeling and acting for these kids where they felt no judgments could be made on them, and thus it precluded institutional work. Inauthentic activity was activity where the students felt they could not risk letting their emotions show, where they could not simply be; it was institutional activity which, meaningful, enjoyable, and satisfying as it might be on its own terms, required them to "play dead" with all that was uncertain, vulnerable, sensitive within themselves—in other words, all that humanized them to themselves, and made them more than simply "wonks" or success-bent performers. Similarly, Ben Snyder found, in work with students at MIT, that the greatest problem of new students was to learn how to stop translating the institution's judgments of their ability into parts of their lives that should never be judged.

Ideas of success and status among middle-level government managers afford another view on the class dimensions of this divide. Such men are found to believe, by and large, that competition and the drive for success are "helpful rather than hurtful," "socially beneficial," and most important, that strong competitiveness is characteristic of people who have "good personalities." Undoubtedly middle-level managers in the private sector would not be differently moved. What is interesting about these attitudes is that below their surface, success and competition turn out to be means, not ends. Through competition, these men see themselves having the power to do things in their lives totally divorced from competition: providing good homes for their families, arriving at a position in work where, once you have proven yourself, you could do things—risky, personally meaningful things—you would not have been permitted to do before. But if this is the case, how do these managers feel about the means, the competitiveness and drive, in and of themselves? They don't, it turns out, think much of pushing or competing as a way of life; few enjoyed demonstrating their worth or, in so doing, putting others in the shade. Was it necessary to be competitive in order to survive on the job? These government employees answered—perhaps differently from those in private industry—that competitiveness was not necessary for sheer day-to-day survival; its use was that it got you to the point where you could really do what *you* wanted, and that made it good.

A feeling that the inner man or woman is absent when you are performing for others is not, then, an exclusive characteristic of manual laborers. Perhaps this inner sense of passivity must necessarily arise whenever a person is making a demonstration of his ability to someone or something outside himself; perhaps the very existence of class authority, of judgment from without oneself and above oneself, draws a circle around human action that human beings always see beyond. However, it is true that the specific actions a man performs to prove himself must have some bearing on the defensive patterns forged by his consciousness.

Let us consider a man like George O'Mora, who used to hammer railroad ties and now polishes floors for a home-cleaning service. The change means a lot to him. Polishing floors is a better job he believes he got, and holds onto, while other workers in the company are fired or laid off, because he is a diligent worker who takes care to do things right. On another level, however, he feels his success on the job to be something that happened *to* him, that his ability there exists at arm's length. What does this feeling do for him? As with O'Malley and the others, it allows him to maintain some feeling of fraternity with his co-workers, for he does worry about not selling out his friends and doing the right thing by other people at work, "no matter who they are or what happens there."

This is not what troubles the college students or governmental managers—the violations of human feeling arising from performing for authority are for them purely personal problems. While for them, as for workingmen, demonstrations of ability do not encompass the fullness of their emotions, the questions of desertion workingmen face are not in their minds.

In a class society, laborers are confronted with the fact that they are treated as a mass, as "nobody special," that they are "run-of-the-mill Americans." These self-definitions are the insistent ones that people who do manual work make of themselves. If being "nobody special" is not awarded much prestige in this society, however, it is a condition which all the nobodies have learned to share. A man or woman within this mass sees humanity both all around and within him- or herself. In contrast to the situation for someone closer to the top, a man near the base of the pyramid who gains approval from those above faces a loss of real dignity. Will he be tempted by his success to act as though his peers not so singled out are no longer worthy of him? A bond of humanity holds him, when he worries about this matter of desertion.

A whole strain of conservative thought from Tocqueville to Ortega y Gasset argues that the "masses" are intolerant of diversity and individual differences out of a fear of being put to shame. Yet it is not a question here of mass psychological pressures toward conformity. It is precisely because being "nobody" carries a certain stigma in this very unequal society that a subtle kind of emotional arrangement has to be made in the life of someone who is "just ordinary" when he does something to distinguish himself. Holding such achievements at arm's length is one such attempt; fragmenting the social information in one's consciousness is another, closely related, defense.

George O'Mora initially appears to the outsider as a man who never makes connections about his experience that the outsider immediately makes. At one point he spoke about his children: "The thing I'm hopeful for is this: they can make whatever they want of themselves. I know I'm never going to stand in their way, I know I'm never going to push them, um . . . they're free . . ." Ten minutes later he was talking about how hard it is for young people to do what they want in terms of work no matter how permissive their parents are, social opportunities having, he believes, dried up. This kind of compartmentalizing of attitudes emerges again and again in George O'Mora's talk; indeed, it characterizes, in one way or another, almost all the figures in this book.

One tends to think of fragmentation in a life as the result of some social disorganization in which the person has been ripped apart. Yet listening to George O'Mora talk, or William O'Malley or Frank Rissarro, one feels a great sense of presence and solidity. Given the fact of being nameless in society, given the ambushes and contradictions of dignity class creates, the more a man's actions are split up in his own mind the less chance he has of being overwhelmed as a whole. Someone like O'Mora is one person in the midst of these contradictions, because *he* has no desire to connect neatly all the parts of himself.

Fragmentation and divisions in the self are the arrangements consciousness makes in response to an environment where respect is not forthcoming as a matter of course.

A VIABLE DEFENSE?

We have tried to show how men can practice alienation in order to maintain equilibrium in their lives, and yet we are troubled about this phenomenon. Hints of something else kept coming out of the interviews, suggestive statements we didn't follow up because we didn't fully grasp what we were hearing—hints that caring and love cannot for long be maintained pure of the world.

These are the hints that return us to the truth of Nietzsche's aphorism. A shop steward in a large electrical plant remarks, "It's a funny thing, when I tell a man or woman they're doing a good job, as likely as not, the next day their work is lousy." Does this mean that, if a person is rewarded for abilities that he or she has decided, on quite logical grounds, to treat as alien to the real self, the reward can seem false or illegitimate, something the person should not have? Frank Rissarro represents an extreme instance: he lies to himself that his successes came because he lied to others; what he has accomplished must be dishonest if he cannot feel he deserves rewards he has received. If the acts performed in a class system are depersonalized, then the benefits and rewards bestowed on the performer may not count in the arena of self-respect, because one has decided not to *let* the performance count.

One of the saddest encounters we had was with a philosophically-minded auto mechanic. A part of him recognizes that he is "deep," as a friend puts it; yet he cannot really accept the fact of his intelligence, since to do so would drag in the status order of the outside society. For, if he is intelligent, why is he a "grease monkey"? He has incisive ideas about why people in filling stations do not often become college professors of philosophy in America, but in talking about himself he makes a break; it is less painful to think he "isn't much, just a part of the woodwork," than to respect his own mind. Such fragmentation gets him by from day to day, but it keeps him a prisoner as well.

More usual is the comment of a factory worker who has an encyclopedic knowledge of sports statistics, makes rapid calculations of batting averages, and the like, but who gets upset when his wife points out his ability: "She shouldn't make anything of it; I mean, I didn't." Why is it so hard for people to say, "I'm good at something"? There is something more here than embarrassment at being praised. The strengths "I" have are not admissible to the arena of ability where they are socially useful; for once admitted, "I"—my real self—would no longer have them.

Once a divorce is effected between love and demonstration of power, what is the strength of love itself? Strong feeling, to be sure, but family love is also a matter of all sorts of actions in a world where power shapes experience, in which mere love does not feed the children or get the money for the vacation. Although the sense of "I" as different from my ability wards off a feeling of being only a role in the institution, it may also leave a man with a sense that his capacity to love gives him no power to deal with the world. The real me who cares, the real me who is sensitive, becomes a vulnerable creature: emotions are an area of self to be shielded, not to be expressed, lest by exposure to the world these tender spots be bruised or hurt.

Carl Dorian's uncle has put this much better than we can:

"Well, yeah, my income goes up just about every year a little more than inflation and taxes, the home is getting more secured, more of the good things . . . but I have this fear, you see what I mean, like it's as though if I want any of these good things then all the good things will go away . . . *See, like if you care about something, you gonna get hurt like as not* . . . I don't let myself hope, I gotta hold back a lot of times from getting involved in how well things are going, you know, the job, what my kids are doing with themselves . . . I don't like it—but I tell you, I get scared if I care too much, I mean if I get all involved and try to get all things working like I want."

A defense that begins as an aid to preserving a man's humanity ends here by isolating his sense of caring so that it appears as something weak and vulnerable, and therefore not to be expressed. The expression of loving feelings becomes a threat; men begin to feel that showing love is synonymous with weakness.

If Nietzsche is right, that power and love have been wrongfully separated in the modern world, it is the class system which has done the wrong. The price of seeing beyond one's institutional role is isolation of love from power. Love then seems a state of consciousness which must be kept secret; a secret is best kept when men do not speak. The pattern consciousness makes out of the social realities of class converts love into a *potential experience* for men, something that goes on in their hearts, but that no one else may know about.

One of the popular images of workingmen concerns the "cult of masculinity" they are supposedly enmeshed in, their emphasis on toughness and hatred of "soft" people.

We think that popular image is largely a glorification of noble savagery, in the manner of D. H. Lawrence. Certainly, the workingmen we knew in Boston do not talk as tough as many advertising people in New York. The image is condescending, but it also presents, though in distorted form, an element of truth; namely, that people who are subject to the power of others, and who feel their dignity compromised by that limitation of freedom, have a tremendous fear of exposing themselves. The world can get at them not so much by telling them what to do as by twisting their feelings of concern around to its own ends—the promotion problem we explored in the last chapter is one example of this. Class, in other words, makes it rational for men to keep their "soft" feelings to themselves until they are very sure they won't be hurt; but in the long wait to be very sure, all sorts of opportunities for expressing affection—opportunities which to the outsider seem safe—may be lost.

We should say that love as a secret appears as a middle-aged phenomenon among the people we knew in Boston; younger factory laborers, in particular, seemed more willing to be vulnerable. The kind of interviewing we did makes such a statement a guess rather than a conclusion from "hard data," but let us give here some of the impressions from a shoe factory on which this view is based.

In the shoe factory, the older workingmen appeared to share intimate feelings with each other much less than the younger ones, although most of the middle-aged workers had been together at the plant for a decade or more. Small things were what these older workers shared—sharing was a ritual of courtesies like getting the morning coffee. But what the older men talked about during coffee break were usually shop matters, seldom home and family or other personal interests. In the outside community, moreover, these older workers replaced fraternal respect with a respect for mutual isolation. "He's a good neighbor, he leaves you alone," was a theme that surfaced again and again.

The break between the generations lies, in this factory, in the desire of younger men and women to get beyond this point in their lives, to translate their inchoate desires for community into reality. If one asks whether the years will wear them down to the retreat of the older men, one really has to ask a larger question: will somehow, someday, the society that makes fraternity so sensitive an issue be altered or destroyed, so that feelings of companionship can find natural expression?

The divided self is like most other kinds of conscious defenses human beings erect for themselves; it stills pain in the short run, but does not remove the conditions that made a defense necessary in the first place. If the defense fails finally to make men happy, or even reconciled, the failure is at worst a sign that men do not have within themselves the power to transcend the world like Nietzsche's gods, that despite an extraordinarily subtle rebalancing of their feelings they cannot escape the influence of a destructive social order.

CHAPTER V

FREEDOM

What does it mean to be free, in a class society? To be unfree, as we've seen, has two meanings: the simpler one is that men cannot do what they want because class circumstances pen them in; the more complicated one involves the idea of compulsion—when institutions make people feel they must prove their dignity by demonstrations of personal ability. The responsibility of self-validation then channels consciousness into the path of sacrifice and betrayal.

The defenses described in the last chapter are a means of conscious struggle against these shackles. In one sense, it could be said, they are men's attempts to be free of the injuries of class. But freedom is not merely freedom *from*, the absence of shackles; freedom is also a more positive conception—the freedom to do a specific thing or live in a specific way. In the present chapter, we want to indicate the positive kind of freedom a class society proposes to its people; in other words, what redemption is offered to keep men from despair?

To explore this question, let us start with an unlikely source: a long-term research project on the relative prestige Americans have assigned over the years to various kinds of work. Investigators at the National Opinion Research Corporation took their first poll on this topic in 1947 and then re-surveyed attitudes in 1963; they were, moreover, able to make comparisons to an earlier study of occupational standing done in 1925. Their results were surprising. Whereas they had expected to see significant shifts in the relative prestige given various jobs, they found instead that over the course of two generations, despite a major depression and substantial changes in the occupational structure, Americans retained a relatively stable picture of what constitutes more prestigious and less prestigious work. But the specific content of these findings is even more interesting than the broad fact that ideas about "good" and "bad" work should have survived in the same form for almost half a century. Here is a summary of NORC's findings:

What Are Desirable Jobs?

Occupation	March, 1947 Rank*	June, 1963 Rank*
U.S. Supreme Ct. Justice	1	1
Physician	2.5	2
Nuclear physicist	18	3.5
Scientist	8	3.5
Government scientist	10.5	5.5
State governor	2.5	5.5
Cabinet member in Fed. Govt.	4.5	8
College professor	8	8

* See footnote on p. 225.

What Are Desirable Jobs?

Occupation	March, 1947 Rank*	June, 1963 Rank*
U.S. representative in Congress	8	8
Chemist	18	11
Lawyer	18	11
Diplomat in U.S. Foreign Service	4.5	11
Dentist	18	14
Architect	18	14
County judge	13	14
Psychologist	22	17.5
Minister	13	17.5
Member of board of directors of large corporation	18	17.5
Mayor of a large city	6	17.5
Priest	18	21.5
Head of a dept. in a state govt.	13	21.5
Civil engineer	23	21.5
Airline pilot	24.5	21.5
Banker	10.5	24.5
Biologist	29	24.5
Sociologist	26.5	26
Instructor in religious school	34	27.5
Captain in the regular army	31.5	27.5
Accountant for a large business	29	29.5
Public school teacher	36	29.5
Owner of a factory that employs about 100 people	26.5	31.5
Building contractor	34	31.5
Artist who paints pictures that are exhibited in galleries	24.5	34.5
Musician in symphony orchestra	29	34.5
Author of novels	31.5	34.5

What Are Desirable Jobs?

Occupation	March, 1947 Rank°	June, 1963 Rank°
Economist	34	34.5
Official of international labor union	40.5	37
Railroad engineer	37.5	39
Electrician	45	39
County agricultural agent	37.5	39
Owner-operator of a printing shop	42.5	41.5
Trained machinist	45	41.5
Farm owner and operator	39	44
Undertaker	47	44
Welfare worker for city govt.	45	44
Newspaper columnist	42.5	46
Policeman	55	47
Reporter on a daily newspaper	48	48
Radio announcer	40.5	49.5
Bookkeeper	51.5	49.5
Tenant farmer—one who owns livestock, machinery and manages the farm	51.5	51.5
Insurance agent	51.5	51.5
Carpenter	58	53
Manager of small store in a city	49	54.5
Local official of labor union	62	54.5
Mail carrier	57	57
Railroad conductor	55	57
Traveling salesman for wholesale concern	51.5	57
Plumber	59.5	59

What Are Desirable Jobs?

Occupation	March, 1947 Rank°	June, 1963 Rank°
Automobile repairman	59.5	60
Playground director	55	62.5
Barber	66	62.5
Machine operator in a factory	64.5	62.5
Owner-operator of a lunch stand	62	62.5
Corporal in the regular army	64.5	65.5
Garage mechanic	62	65.5
Truck driver	71	67
Fisherman who owns own boat	68	68
Clerk in a store	68	70
Milk route man	71	70
Streetcar motorman	68	70
Lumberjack	73	72.5
Restaurant cook	71	72.5
Singer in a nightclub	74.5	74
Filling station attendant	74.5	75
Dockworker	81.5	77.5
Railroad section hand	79.5	77.5
Night watchman	81.5	77.5
Coal miner	77.5	77.5
Restaurant waiter	79.5	80.5
Taxi driver	77.5	80.5
Farmhand	76	83
Janitor	85.5	83
Bartender	85.5	83
Clothes presser in laundry	83	85
Soda fountain clerk	84	86
Sharecropper—one who owns no livestock or equipment and does not manage farm	87	87
Garbage collector	88	88

What Are Desirable Jobs?

Occupation	March, 1947 Rank*	June, 1963 Rank*
Street sweeper	89	89
Shoe shiner	90	90

* These ratings were based on the responses given to the question: "For each job mentioned, please pick out the statement (excellent, good, average, somewhat below average, or poor) that best gives *your own personal opinion* of the general standing that such a job has." The numbers are an attempt to give an idea of the relative strength of response in evaluating each of these ninety occupations. The relative prestige of these occupations was ranked in the same way, by people of all classes.

This prestige scale shows clearly that occupational status is *not* the same thing as direct economic power or the power to command others. A member of the board of a large corporation ranks significantly lower than the lawyer, dentist, or college professor, yet he holds greater power to control the resources of society. The banker, a man with similar power in the corporate structure, is even further down the list, while the owner of a factory that employs a hundred people does not even rank in the top third of prestigious occupations. The same is to some extent true of politicians: a college professor on this scale has more prestige than a city mayor, a scientist more than a U.S. representative. Let us try to explain why, in light of the injuries of class, the NORC findings should come out in this way.

INTERPRETIVE WORK
AND NURTURANCE

In general, the top third of this scale is dominated by those who are involved in various interpretative functions in society. Professionals are supposed to possess expertise at interpreting how and why things happen; their knowledge is of a different order from the capacity to wage corporate struggles or successful campaigns for office. This ordering of status, where men do not respect most those whom they must obey, is by no means unique to the last four decades, or to the age of industrial capitalism; at very diverse times and places in human history this same premium has been placed on nurturance over power.

Roughly the same hierarchy of values appears, for instance, in a myth of ancient India, composed over a thousand years before the birth of Christ, explaining the origins of, and the justification for, the caste system. According to this myth the universe began with the sacrifice of a god-man, Purusha, whose body was divided into what were to become the major social orders of Indian society, hierarchically arranged. Purusha's mouth became the priests, thinkers, lawgivers, judges, and ministers of state; his two arms became the nobility, kings, vassals, and warriors; his two thighs, the landowners, merchants, moneylenders; and from his two feet arose the workers, artisans, and serfs.

The priests of ancient India, like their European counterparts in the Middle Ages, were often the only literate men of their time. Their vision and knowledge, a mystery to other men, were supposed to give them the power to propitiate the gods and influence natural forces. Operating thus as mediators between the gods and man, the priests were therefore considered to stand above other men, closer to the gods.

The modern counterpart of the priest is the professional;

Vladimir Nabokov chose his words well when he called Sigmund Freud the "witch-doctor from Vienna." The physician interprets your body to you, he has knowledge that you do not have, but that you need to survive. Scientists—chemists, biologists, physicists—likewise are the interpreters of natural forces which determine the survival of human society. Psychologists and clergymen are the interpreters of psychic and spiritual forces, of who you are to yourself, to others, and to the gods; judges, lawyers, and legislators are the givers, interpreters, and prescribers of the social order. All professionals, then, are priests: they interpret mysteries which affect the lives of those who do not understand.

Since the power of professionals lies in their ability to give or withhold knowledge, they are in positions that by and large are not questioned by others; they are "authorities" themselves, "authorities" unto themselves. It is precisely the endowment of a professional with this inner, self-sufficing power that gives him a higher status than men with economic power. For the autonomy makes him seem "market-proof," in that he can perform his function no matter what is happening to others around him.° His nurturing power appears as an ability that he brings *to* people; they need him in a way that he does not need them. It is in this sense that he is the only truly independent man in a class society—he is needed more than he needs.

If the value placed on interpretative over organizational

° This is one reason why the disappearance of engineering jobs in 1969–70 caused such severe emotional disorganization among the engineers laid off; they had never expected that professionals like themselves could ever be thrown into the industrial job market in that way—i.e., that their skills might ever be unneeded.

power has a sweep beyond modern class society, the actual power of a nurturer, a professional, intersects those values of independence and freedom from market exchange that have acquired great importance in the United States during its industrial century.

The American individualist was traditionally an independent proprietor or farmer. In the early nineteenth century, when the United States was a nation of small farmers and shopkeepers, there was indeed a reasonable chance for a man to become his own boss. But the possibility of realizing this dream has faded with time. Early in the last century, eighty percent of the employed white population were self-employed; by 1870 the percentage had dropped to forty-one. In 1940 only eighteen percent were self-employed, and by 1967, only half that number, nine percent, were in this way independent.*

Nonetheless, among blue-collar workers self-employment has persisted as an image of freedom that will remove the tensions they presently encounter. Chinoy's study of auto workers in a medium-sized Midwestern city in the 1950's showed that many of those who came to work at the auto plant thought of their jobs as only temporary, as a kind of way station before they could strike out on their own. By the time many of these workers were in their late twenties or early thirties, they no longer viewed their jobs as temporary; yet their aspirations remained. The persistence among middle-aged workers of this particular dream of a gas station or small store or farm of one's own can perhaps be explained by the fact that these are about the only forms of

* Figures from Bottomore, Bonnell, and Reich, already cited.

self-employment open to those with little formal education. Against this old ideal, however, a new one has been laid, a compelling dream among the people we interviewed of what their children could become.

The middle-aged people we interviewed did not speak about the good life for their children in terms of small business. It exists, most of them believe, in the professions, in medicine or college teaching or architecture, in occupations where the child makes use of his or her intellectual powers. The NORC studies cited above involved interviews with people of all social classes; the value placed on nurturant work was expressed in our interviews so strongly that manual workers at the very least fit the general trend. For workers, however, these desires have even less chance of realization than do those of becoming a proprietor or farmer: only about eighteen out of every thousand sons of manual laborers enter the professions.° In the face of this reality, why does the dream persist?

The reason the dream is so strong is that only in the professions does the man of action, exerting his abilities, appear united with the real self. Only the professional has the kind of power that would permit him to carry out Nietzsche's injunction to unite love and power. Such a man appears to be able to express his care to others without fear of affront because they need that nurturance from him, and he has no need of any product or action in return to practice his art, save their submission to his will—a submission the patient in

° Even fewer reach the penultimate position of self-employed professional: about eight out of one thousand males from a manual-laboring background do so. Computed from Blau and Duncan, *The American Occupational Structure* (New York: John Wiley & Sons; 1967).

need of treatment, the client accused of a crime, the student in need of knowledge or a grade, does not refuse. This one-way street is freedom.

Let us give a concrete instance of what this idea of control feels like, for a young man who talks about entering the "profession" of computer salesman—and whose ideas of control, by the way, reveal why he considers it a profession.

Patrick Flanagan is a young man from an Irish working-class neighborhood in Boston who has made it to a college out West. The son of a shipping clerk, he takes pride in his accomplishments so far, especially when he compares them with those of other boys from his old school and neighborhood. He spent the first hour we talked with him in a careful account of how he had moved in each grade further from the community of his parents, through long hours of study and perseverance. Flanagan measures his success in very personal terms, in terms of self-liberation, in chances for new pleasures and new insights, in a chance to be understood by people he believes as competent as himself. All these opportunities have led him to share a liberal politics he proudly associates with the "really capable people" from upper-class homes. He is against the Vietnam war and talks of new life-styles associated with the student movement. "It's the same thing you fellows feel," he said to the interviewer, who was himself a neatly dressed college student with long hair.

He needs above all, he says, to be free of being bossed around by or having to deal with "dull insensitive types," to shake free of "those stupid people."

Flanagan comes across as a very cynical young man, yet the fashions of disillusion have not entirely taken hold of him. Asked what his plans were for the future, he replied,

"I've taken a strong interest in computers; I also like to think about means of persuasion and things like that." His dream is to start his own sales agency, and with characteristic zeal, he has formed a spare-time partnership with a friend for free-lance work. After a long session of protesting the shackles imposed by blind authority, discussing his discovery of and then resistance to the manipulation he felt practiced on him by his schooling, his family, and American culture as a whole, he began to talk of making manipulation his own lifework with no sense of moral contradiction, no feeling of inconsistency.

What precisely is the appeal of selling high-technology goods? "I want to get into a position where the freaks like Agnew can't get me," he says. "I want to get enough know-how so nobody can tell me what to do." Flanagan uses expressions like "being my own boss," and metaphors that connote getting out from under the domination of higher authority, to describe his dream of independence. In this his feelings are continuous with the desires of the auto workers Ely Chinoy interviewed for, say, a gas-station franchise of their own. Flanagan is similarly thinking about what kind of work, today, will permit him to escape from having to take orders. His answer to the working-class Irish community in which he had to live, with its "deadening stupidity," is to reverse the power situation so that through his work *he* manipulates *others*, because he knows something special. He makes an explicit connection between being intelligent and being in control on these terms: "You got to be smart to get a hold of what other people are feeling, and mold it; that's the appeal to me."

But Flanagan's dream for his future is more than a desire

to escape, more than a desire for revenge: "Once I get into a position like that, I can really be me, really do some good, because whatever I think *should* happen, it'll at least be all on my own shoulders to make it happen." Independence, freedom on the terms of class society, opens up the possibility to him of a more genuine expression of caring for others. Only when he is in a position to exercise special abilities, only then, can he act according to his feelings.

By idealizing professional work in this way, Patrick Flanagan is trying to deal with the problems, discussed in the last chapter, involved in the real self being safe only as a secret, safe only as an intention, but unsafe and vulnerable when expressed. The assistant school principal, it will be recalled, acts sternly because he is afraid that the students may use him or mock him if he, a figure of power, shows softness and tenderness toward them. If Anna Baron shows love for her parents, will they take it as a sign that she is ready to return to the fold, and will she then defer to them in the old ways?

In actual social interaction, people know what they see before them: you are a whole person to me, and I judge you on this basis, not on the basis of something you try usually to keep hidden. I may be dimly aware of it, I may sense that you are doing to *your*self what I practice within *my*self, yet I would be taking a terrible risk to act on that intuition, to expose myself to you. We are working in a factory or sitting in the same classroom or together at a union meeting; you say something that seems like an opening to friendship, but it is all disguised, it comes in between the lines of what you are saying, because overt declarations leave you too exposed. Shall I act on my imagining of the substance of your soul when I can't see it, or shall we get on with business?

Sometimes, of course, people do make the leap, do act on faith, and find themselves rewarded by others. But in a guarded society where the realities of power have penetrated the intimacies of experience, a man can be rebuffed only so many times before he finds it safer to act on emotionally neutral terms. If this is true of social equals, how much more is it true of those who are of unequal class, of a high school principal or teacher dealing with his students, a laborer with his foreman.

For the professional, by contrast, nothing needs to be hidden because his work makes him invulnerable to rebuffs. This idealization, however, is still tied to the world of power and performance. Patrick Flanagan's idea of selling complex, mysterious machines so that he can live a life of action in accordance with the sensitive, feeling being he feels imprisoned within him is a construction of what would make this unified self possible in a world where class keeps action and feeling apart. The real self is permitted to be a reality only if you can manipulate others for what you believe is their own good.

In our interviews the attraction of the professions was divorced from the behavior of concrete professionals. It is the position in which the doctor or university professor is placed relative to other people that makes these occupations seem so valuable. We asked a mother of three, for instance, why she wanted her eldest boy to become a doctor, when her family is deeply in debt for medical bills and her experiences with gynecologists have been an unending series of horror stories. "It's not the money, see . . . if you could be in a position like that, at least nothing stands in the way of your doing good . . . that's what you're there for . . . if you're a good person, then you can be a good doctor, and—I

233

think such a person ought to treasure that, don't you? I mean, most people can't act like that . . ." The position seems a road to the unification of the self: "If you're a good person, then you can be a good doctor."

Here is the basis for understanding why the workingpeople we talked to made—as they did—a distinction in their feelings about their employers and political leaders, on the one hand, and professors, intellectuals, and students on the other. About their employers and about politicians, people showed a tough and cynical attitude, in which a recognition of power was mixed with little awe. "An executive is just a hustler who knew the right people," remarked one man; other people spoke with distrust of a woman from the old community who had risen through politics. In sum, people often showed recognition of such achievement without admiration for it.

We found intense resentment against intellectuals and students as well, but it was of a wholly different kind. What workingpeople hated to see was students acting as if they didn't care about the freedom that was open to them, as if they were wasting themselves when others so desperately wanted the chance for control over their lives that they had. This resentment can exist only when the position itself is idealized, so that the person in that position is like a priest who betrays his office. Similarly, Fred Gorman, the TV repairman cited earlier, feels no surprise at the machinations down at City Hall, but is seriously affronted when he sees those two engineers changing TV tubes: they had an enviable position, yet they seem to refuse to sit upon the throne. If *they* refuse, is there any escape at all, any hope for a healing of the breach that has opened in Gorman's own life?

This may seem to professionals a romanticized way to look at the professions, but it closely resembles the middle-class romanticizing of the Artist and his Calling that began in the nineteenth century. In both cases, a small, elite group of people appear to others as fully developed human beings. Just as the artist in the last century was celebrated by the middle classes as a vital man, in touch with his passions, so now does the professional seem to another class the only kind of man who can unite love and power. Although the nature of the idealized figure has changed, the unity across time is that in a class society there is room for only a few to seem fully self-developed.

FREEDOM IN MANUAL WORK

The terms in which people form an image of who is elite, and why, are also the terms in which workingmen evaluate freedom closer to home, in judging good and bad kinds of manual and lower-status white-collar labor. Let us go back to the NORC scale for a moment. It appears that much blue-collar work commands *more* prestige than various kinds of white-collar work. The manager of a small store in a city has about the same standing as a carpenter but ranks lower than an electrician. A carpenter, however, has more prestige than a traveling salesman for a wholesale concern or a store clerk.

The reason for this intermixing of white- and blue-collar work is, we think, that people measure the status of the ordinary occupations just as they measure status at the top. Occupations in which the individual possesses some degree of autonomy—that is, some degree of freedom from authority and from having to define his own function in terms of the shifting demands of others—are more desirable than jobs where a person has to deal with others and respond to them. Thus, a carpenter can feel he is doing a good job when he makes a smooth joint working by himself, but a store manager can do a good job only when other people buy. The manager may make twice as much money, but, as the NORC scale shows, people see the carpenter as having a better job.

This reasoning explains why at the bottom end of the scale are found not factory jobs but service jobs where the individual has to perform personally for someone else. A bartender is listed below a coal miner, a taxi driver below a truck driver; we believe this occurs because their functions are felt to be more dependent on, and more at the mercy of, others.

The values that determine the relative status given to jobs influence as well the actual satisfactions men and women can have within any one category of work. The last chapter mentioned Blauner's finding that the more autonomy a worker has in regulating the time for his duties, the happier and less alienated he feels in performing them. Other studies of work-isolated versus people-involving jobs show that those who work alone find more satisfaction in their labor than those who must deal with other people. Indeed, in the latter study, it was found that people who had to manage subordinates felt less satisfaction in their jobs, and felt they had less status, than colleagues who worked alone and did not have such a responsibility for other people's performance.

In general, then, a higher ranking is given to those who can perform in isolation, who do not need or depend on others. Increased status in the American industrial order thus appears as an increase in individualistic behavior, in a flight from rubbing upon or against others in the economic terms of market exchange. The great paradox here is that people are then conceived to be able to give to others, to provide nurturance and help, only when they are insulated from others, only when their abilities become "innate" skills by virtue of talent and training, only when they bring help to others rather than develop their helping powers in interaction and exchange.

As bureaucracy and interdependence grow, as the giant corporation replaces the small business, as an increasing division of labor takes place, one would think that more and more people would be deprived of work situations where they can experience autonomy. But the very division of labor creates the possibility for numerous isolated niches in the job structure where people can try to make of their position an island cut off by expertise from other people. We are thinking here of the growing attempts to "professionalize" many jobs, particularly in corporate bureaucracies and managerial posts. Melvin Kohn argues that this process occurs because bureaucratic workers have more job security and the jobs themselves are more complex. But these circumstances do not explain the desire itself to professionalize.

Leonard Sayles writes that, instead, "the manager wants to move into a position in the structure in which the balance of initiations favors him," where he is insulated enough so that it is he who can request obedience from others, rather than they from him. If one can convince others that one's skills are unique, that one is the expert whose decisions cannot be challenged, then one can become insulated from the commands of others.

Much of this professionalizing, to be sure, involves arbitrary mystification: complex language for simplicities, elaborate bureaucratic routine where direct action would work as well or better, and so on. But these charades are necessary if the bureaucrat is to escape what is happening to George Corona, the supervisor who, as we saw, feels dishonored by his responsibility for those below him. For the more interdependent work in corporations and bureaucracies grows, the more does productive work on the bottom get entangled with administration and office processing, and the more white-collar workers get enmeshed with responsibility for the performance of lower-level functionaries or plant workers. That is what happened to Corona, and the only way out is to do what Patrick Flanagan wants to do: make the "balance of initiatives" flow to you by a professionalizing of your skill so that you are necessary to others but they cannot understand what you do.

Merely to condemn this as phony misses the meaning of the situation to the people involved.

". . . Now a college professor, he's got to be really smart or he can't work—take you, now, you seem like a nice boy, but nice boys don't get too far, right? . . . You got to have what it takes, you got to have brains, you know, like you're worth something . . ."

"Look, it's very simple. I'm a man, you're a man, right? So we talk, I drink your beer, we communicate, like they say. But we walk out of this house, people say about you, 'He's got something to him'; they see me, they say hello if they know me, otherwise they walk past . . . Now I don't mind, the worms'll get to us all in the end, but *you* never have to worry about yourself 'cause you got it in you to do right."

This garbage man is not just reacting to a power he sees *in* the interviewer. Intelligence also becomes the capacity to explain and to throw light upon power itself. As we observed in the last chapter, it is characteristic of institutions in making both good and bad personal judgments to act mystifyingly. Nobody, however, is going to "mystify" a doctor or an architect about whether he does good work or not. He is his own judge, for good or ill, because he is the only one who really knows what he does.

Among people whose work does not involve interpretation, however, to believe the position of doctors is to increase feelings of absolute dependency on them, and similarly on the professionals in other areas which are of general human importance: housing, political rights, education. Who are *they*, these factory hands, these janitors, in the face of people whose job it is to make things better, by explaining the layman to himself. How can the workers' own perceptions of their needs be legitimate? That is the problem for the middle-aged electrician who was being displaced from his home by a university. Remember that his anger is capped by a putdown of himself: "I mean, you can't stand in the way of progress . . . It's probably better in the long run that this thing is happening, I mean, I *know* they didn't need to take this street, but they probably got their good reasons." It is because professionals hold knowledge which is considered universal, and needed in daily life, that they have a legitimacy which the electrician whose expertise concerns only transistors does not feel in himself.

This dream of autonomous work does not involve a revolt against the class system. It is an attempt to flee from being judged, to be sure, to flee the anxieties of the market in which a man is put up on the block and assayed. But in order to become "market-proof," you have to be so good, so developed inside, that nobody could refuse to buy you. The manipulative overtones in this idea of autonomous work parallel Andrew Carnegie's strategy in forming a steel company: corner some essential productive function and you dictate your own terms. The dream of autonomous work idealized by the professional has, of course, a more beneficent end in view than Carnegie's enterprise—becoming a doctor is seen as worthwhile because then humane feeling and personal power are united. But the means to that end form a kind of psychological cartel.

Society, however, denies workingpeople much chance of moving into elite professional jobs, and that denial has something to do, finally, with the concept of time embodied in this idea of freedom.

FREEDOM AS REBIRTH

In an early English fantasy of a tanner in heaven talking to God upon His throne, the tanner speaks with a Cockney accent, uses imperfect grammar, makes jokes, and otherwise conducts himself as he had in the world down below where he sweated fourteen hours a day mixing dye, and God loves him for what he is. In a state of regeneration, so runs this early story, the worker would still recognize himself, would remain with the personal character he had on earth.

Modern dreams of autonomy, however, make a man unrecognizable to himself: doctors talk differently than plumbers, and by extension the children of plumbers who become doctors talk differently. By changing your personal actions, by developing capacities within yourself, you change your social circumstances in this dream; but you are then cut off from the creature who needed to dream of freedom.

The consequence of this rebirth is ironic: autonomy is a state in which the inner and the outer man become one, but the man himself disappears. In this position of being free to be yourself, the weight of your experience will be lost, and between the man who you want to be and the you who has suffered there is no continuity.

William James, in *The Varieties of Religious Experience,* speaks of a "second birth" that occurs in many religious conversions. This is a feeling of a new self emerging which begins to act according to ethical emotions. The birth of the new self is preceded, as in St. Augustine's *Confessions,* by a traumatic period in which the individual *wants* to act much differently, but feels held back by circumstances beyond his control. How far does the dream of autonomy, then, resemble a religious conversion?

We should say first that in our interviews, we found organized religion little on the minds of workingmen, and all attempts to raise the issue in relation to work, feelings of personal adequacy, and the like, fell flat. As far as we could tell, both men and women thought of their religion as a distinct compartment of their lives, as an obligatory role separate from the obligations of class.

In any event it is not the religion of established churches that creates class feelings. It is rather that the social system creates tensions that can *only* be resolved through drastic changes in the self. This is the weight of class—a weight that can be lifted only by transformations of the self comparable to those described in earlier eras by words like redemption or salvation. And yet the class structure creates as the ideal toward which self-transformation aims something quite different from the ideal Augustine sought after. He sought not so much to leave the world, not so much a redemption "from," as James put it, as a union with the Deity, a redemption "towards." Autonomous work, however, does not make men dream of a class-less society, of a redemption towards; the change in self implied by "professionalizing" one's self keeps one still immersed in the old world but no longer exposed to its wounding power.

This takes on a larger meaning when we contrast this modern dream of a unified self to the role religion played among English factory laborers of the new industrial cities at the turn of the nineteenth century. E. P. Thompson, in his superb *The Making of the English Working-Class*, argues that, as hopes grew among these early industrial workers for bettering their lot through collective action, there resulted a waning of their belief in redemption in a world after death. Redemption after death was replaced by *collective* salvation in this world. However, during periods where the prospects for collective action in this world seemed dim, individuals returned to religion, to find in the life after death a promise for themselves alone. By contrast, redemption in our times glorifies the loving man as a man alone, in this world. Unlike the early English worker seeking God's aid, the redeemed man now will unify himself; he measures his redemption by how little he needs to depend on others in order to care for them.

CONCLUSION

A FLAWED
HUMANISM

CONCLUSION

In the craft guilds of Venice, Florence, and other centers of the Italian Renaissance, a distinctive idea of ability in work took hold. By 1450, competition for individual praise and recognition of their work had reached a frenzied point among silversmiths, leather workers, and weavers, as well as among sculptors and court painters. It would have seemed absurd then, however, to think of a dignified man being reflected in his ability to make a good piece of jewelry. The investment a craftsman made in his work was just the opposite: what he created would establish his repute independent of his person, the jewelry or silver perhaps keeping his name alive after his death. As silversmith or weaver, it was the object that held of him what he wanted to make public.

Today, the idea of ability has become a wholly different phenomenon. Excellence in the object is only a means to measuring excellence in the person. The demonstration of worth now has become a demonstration about inner capacity in the man greater than his tangible works, about a virtue which permits him to transcend situation after situation, mastering each but attached and identified with none.

A peculiar idea of efficiency is connected to this disembodied excellence. Having to act in concert with others means a person has to respond to them, and these relations may so entangle men with one another that a judge could not tell whom to reward for the work, nor could the entangled individual really feel he had a chance to show what he alone could do. If ability is a demonstration about you, rather than a Renaissance-like investment of yourself in an object, then the more you have to act together with other people, the less chance you have to be rewarded for emerging from the mass—which is the social definition of ability itself. While labor grows every day more interdependent, the dream of independent action remains strong because it seems the only way to show that *you* accomplish things.

The irony is that a man who seeks to display his talents as efficiently as possible feels held back by others, and yet it is toward establishing his worthiness to be respected by others that all this concentrated striving is directed.

We are arguing here against ability organized in this form, not against being good at something as an automatic evil in itself. The plea we feel runs through all the lives presented in this book is to be relieved of having to prove oneself this way, to gain a hold instead on the innate *meaningfulness* of actions. Since it is impossible to return to the city-state that brought the Renaissance idea of ability into being, how can the weight of class be lifted now?

DENIALS OF DIGNITY
BY CASTE AND CLASS

In a letter to a friend, Madame de Sévigné writes about a hanging she witnessed one morning. It was striking, she records, to see the condemned man trembling during the preliminaries of the execution, when he was only a common peasant. He groaned and wailed incessantly, causing some amusement among the ladies and gentlemen come to see the spectacle; once hoisted up, his body wriggling in the noose, he presented, Madame de Sévigné remarked, a most remarkable sight.

The modern reader feels only horror at the callousness of this description. Yet Madame de Sévigné was not a vicious woman by the standards of the late seventeenth century. She, like other aristocrats of her circle, could view hangings with disinterested fascination, because the person being killed was a creature whose inner nature had little relation to her own. As good Christians, the highborn had of course to believe that all men were equal in the sight of God, but fortunately He had not gone to the extreme of demanding that they look at things among themselves in quite the same way. When the word "caste" is applied to the *ancien régime* in Europe, it refers, beyond all barriers of custom and hereditary right, to the notion that people of different social stations belong to different species, that the humanity or worthiness of a duchess has little relationship to the kind of humanity accessible to the common peasant. The corollary —explicitly stated in another letter of Madame de Sévigné's—is that the "humbling" of inferiors is necessary to the maintenance of social order.

"Humbling," however, is the most routine of modern occurrences, and it may be wondered if perhaps what we have seen in this book is the continuance of the morality of caste, with its wounding image of the dignity of man, in a society without hereditary rights, without an aristocracy of leisure,

or kings. Yet the trials through which the workingpeople of
Boston have passed they would never have known in Madame de Sévigné's time, nor would their inner uneasiness be
a product of the callousness towards the common people
shown by this woman who within her own circle was sym-
pathetic and sensitive. Their problems result from a society
in which unequal social strata exist, but in which the lines
between the groups are permeable, permeable through the
exercise of distinctive personal ability.

The possibility of a peasant proving himself worthy of his
master's respect as an equal was unknown in the France of
Louis Quatorze and Madame de Sévigné; social mobility between castes did occasionally occur, but it never acquired
the modern connotation of removing a stain on one's dignity. Though peasants humbled by the elite may have
suffered as much as Ricca Kartides, the janitor whose children were ordered off the apartment house lawn, their redemption was to come in the life after death where noble
and serf would stand as equals before God.

All the dreams of individuality now, all the anger and accusations, revolve around the issue of a common dignity.
The workingpeople of Boston have been denied the *presumption*, rather than the *possibility*, of societal respect, denied some way of moving through daily life without being
defensive and on guard, some way of being open with other
people without being hurt. The humbling of today is as oppressive as that of the *ancien régime*, but of a different kind:
it is at once less brutal and more insidious.

Perhaps the subtlety that marks off this modern humbling
most from the manners of the past revolves around questions of family love. That a duke should feel distant from a

field hand was hardly the ground on which the peasant could feel himself to be an unworthy mate for someone of his own station. But in a society where the stations are permeable, what a father like William O'Malley or Ricca Kartides has to give his family appears to him to be very much a matter of how much acceptance he can win in the outer world. These men love their wives and children as people to people, and want their love returned in the same classless way. They are afraid that what they have to give for love, however, depends on their standing in the larger world. It is in this way that the permeability of social strata, an abstract condition far from the daily life of a father and his son, still intrudes into his life, so that he feels vulnerable at the times when he wants to give to the boy.

The injustices of class have traditionally been attacked on the grounds that the deck is stacked, that the rich are more likely to be rewarded than the poor, that the inequalities of wealth are undeserved. Initially this critique seems to be a good way to show what in a class society leads to the feelings portrayed in this book. The teachers in the Watson School, seeking to make their teaching rewarding when they fear their charges will be resistant, "arbitrarily" select a few to mold in their own image. The managers of the auto factory, of the clerical pool, of the electronics plant, must act arbitrarily in trying to decide whom to promote, when more are qualified than can be rewarded. The self-blame that workers arrive at in order to make sense of these actions seems also arbitrary; the children are not stupid, nor do they think of themselves as stupid as long as they are not forced to compare themselves with those few of whom the institution approves. Carl Dorian likes his work, William O'Malley feels gratified by working well and hard, as long as they do not have to prove themselves in front of a superior.

The word "arbitrary," however, threatens to mislead. It suggests that if we could only work out the matter through employee group therapy, alternate leisure activities, or some similar approach, we could get people to the point where they didn't take their place in society so seriously, and, in the words of one management consultant, "make people feel that if they can't be president, they can still have a good time."

Even more, the word "arbitrary" threatens to mislead because it suggests that the wrong individuals are getting the rewards. A class society is one in which people do not get what they deserve by virtue of what they produce; the formula seems so simple, and yet it is so pervertible, for what does "deserving" mean? From the time careers first became open to talent toward the end of the eighteenth century, class society has had a very simple answer to this accusation of injustice. If you have sufficient merit, you rise up through the structure of classes till you reach the level of society your talents permit. The readers of Horatio Alger were never presented with the factory slums as a decent life—no pretense of justifying poverty was made. These things are terrible, true, but you see that at least some people escape them, and the reason they do is because they are smart, have pluck and nerve; if you don't like poverty, you too can leave it *if* you are good enough.

Workingmen intellectually reject the idea that endless opportunity exists for the competent. And yet, the institutions of class force them to apply the idea to themselves: if *I* don't escape being part of the woodwork, it's because I didn't develop my powers enough. Thus, talk about how arbitrary a class society's reward system is will be greeted with general agreement—with the proviso that in my own case I should have made more of myself.

Once that proviso is added, challenging class institutions becomes saddled with the agonizing question, Who am I to make the challenge? To speak of American workers as having been "bought off" by the system or adopting the same conservative values as middle-class suburban managers and professionals, is to miss all the complexity of their silence and to have no way of accounting for the intensity of pent-up feeling that pours out when workingpeople do challenge higher authority.

Surely, however, the peculiar inheritance of our country—a set of public beliefs about the common dignity of man—ought to serve as a rebuke to all the injustices and denials of class. Surely, a nation's public philosophy, founded on the idea that all men have equal claims on each other's respect, should provide a shield of belief for people; surely this public philosophy ought to work against inferring a man's dignity from his social standing.

A FLAWED HUMANISM

At the end of Madame de Sévigné's generation, a small but influential group of writers were revolted by the human consequences of the old ideas of caste. Their rebellion took form as a defense of the most defenseless members of society, children in schools and adults in prisons. Cesare Beccaria examined the prisons of Italy and France in the 1720's and discovered that men were chained by the neck for twenty years as punishment for petty theft; no matter what their "civil condition," he wrote, this was unacceptable treatment. A long line of eighteenth-century humanists attacked the schools run by priests, Diderot for one being unable to understand why lashes of the whip enhanced the study of Latin or of Christian ethics. Within a short time, the condemnation of physical cruelty passed into a condemnation of all social situations where men were made vulnerable by arbitrary law or custom. Voltaire, for instance, attacked courts where a man could be thrown into prison not on the basis of what he had done, but on intimations that he might be a devil.

The outrage of these men was considered a strange aberration at the time. People of the greatest delicacy and refinement were accustomed to harsh measures directed at the mass below, whose brutish nature was thought to need strong reins. You accuse me of inhumanity and I ask you what you can possibly mean, when I treat my family with affection, my servants with firmness, and my rulers with loyal deference. In the face of this, it was a question for Diderot or Beccaria of finding a rationale for their own anger.

It was among this generation of reformers that a definite notion about the relationship between human dignity and compassion for men took form which has passed down into the public ideals of our time. The Enlightenment humanists came to believe that *caritas* in the world was demanded, not by the dictates of an unseen God, but by a common worldly power among men. The right to decent treatment came from a power of rational thinking that ran throughout the human species and in fact defined what it was to be a man. In Diderot's *Encyclopedia*, for example, the section on

"Art" excludes almost all discussion of court painting and sculpture and concentrates on the tools and products of manual laborers. Instead of people becoming more "noble" in the moral sense the higher their caste, he and his fellows saw the web of human merit running through all men in the society. Where the Renaissance philosopher Pico della Mirandola believed extraordinary men struggled to rise above the ordinary to produce the achievements of civilization, Enlightenment writers like Voltaire believed the capacity for civilized achievement to lie within the grasp of any member of the human race, if only he could develop the rational powers nature had instilled in him.

Most Enlightenment humanists never intended to preach a doctrine of equality in social conditions. They preached to the powerful of the old regime, arguing that bonds of respect must cut across the old castes. Indeed, we find one of the *Encyclopédistes* muttering as he is being led to the scaffold during the French Revolution, "Vicious, vicious levelers, you have betrayed reason in the name of equality."

The modern belief in social equality does, however, flow directly from the union of human compassion with the recognition of the potential power all men have to perform acts of reasoning and understanding. For if I am an ordinary man, and yet have within me a power of intellection like that of my lord, how do I make sense of the social separation between us? If I let the dream of a common dignity grow strong in me, then I want the barriers of privilege removed so that I can develop this potential.

This unintended consequence of Enlightenment humanism ought to be a standing rebuke to the inequities in the present industrial order. The ideal ought to provide those who are, or feel themselves to be, powerless with a simple, potent weapon with which to make sense of their condition: I am weak in the face of the Sirs of the world, they control my life, they make me feel ashamed as well as angry. But these things are *their* doing, their tricks. I know I have the potential within me to be as good as they; I won't take it. This is cause for anger, it demands joining together with others to rebel . . . And yet the belief alone is no comfort, under what appear to be very different conditions.

A Russian street-sweeper, an ardent believer in communism, tells an interviewer he does not personally "matter as much as a Party member"; German office workers are reported often to feel "humiliated" by their clothes; American construction workers tell a team of researchers they feel they have to give their sons cars in order to be respected as fathers. Without his possessions, every man walks with pride, preached the Abbé de Sieyès in 1790, but these workingmen and women of the modern world are not so sure. Just being a human being seems to them a state in which they are vulnerable; "I suppose I am not as dignified," the Russian remarks, "as people with more power and influence."

What these workers are saying is that the dignity of man is not *believable* as the Abbé de Sieyès preached it, even as they want to believe in themselves and have others respect them, even as they are outraged when others treat them like "part of the woodwork." Man alone, without making a demonstration of his worth, by just *being*, appears to them to be a vulnerable creature.

One of the reasons class makes the doctrine of the Abbé de Sieyès unbelievable is that his humanism, and that of the other Enlightenment writers of both Right and Left, has a flaw at its very center. The humanists banished the courts of appeal beyond the world, they banished higher authority whose power is unlike the powers of men—all these old notions are put away as enslaving superstition. The humanists effected a juncture between respect among men and a *potential* power all men had in the world. That is a fateful and risky step, as Nietzsche saw, for what happens to the mutual respect when men enact the potential within them? When the common potential is expressed in dissimilar ways? Surely those who are the most intelligent or able or competent have demonstrated more character in manifesting a potential that flows through all; don't they therefore deserve to be treated with more respect than others, or at least to be entrusted with more power? This would be only reasonable, after all; they showed themselves to be better in practice when all began the same.

If I believe that the man I call "Sir" and who calls me by my first name started with an equal fund of powers, do not our differences, do not all the signs of courtesy and attention given to him but denied me, do not his very feelings of being different in "taste" and understanding from me, show that somehow he has developed his insides more than I mine? How else can I explain inequalities? The institutions may be structured so that he wins and I lose, but this is my life, this is thirty or forty years of being alive that I am talking about, and what I have experienced in school, and at work, is that people are supposed to understand what happens to them in life in terms of what they make of themselves. I see this man, who I know is no better than I, being treated better by others—even I treat him that way. Much as I know it isn't right, much as I rebel against his putting on airs and trying to act superior, there is a secret self-accusation implanted in me by my very belief in our basic equality. Even though we might have been born in different stations, the fact that he is getting more means that somehow he had the power in him, the character, to "realize himself," to earn his superiority.

It is in this way that a system of unequal classes is actually reinforced by the ideas of equality and charity formulated in the past. The idea of potential equality of power has been given a form peculiarly fitted to a competitive society where *in*equality of power is the rule and expectation. If all men start on some basis of equal potential ability, then the inequalities they experience in their lives are *not* arbitrary, they are the logical consequence of different personal drives to use those powers—in other words, social differences can now appear as questions of character, of moral resolve, will, and competence.

The lesson of this historic flaw is that once respect is made the reward for human ability, no matter if the ability is seen potentially in all, the stage is set for all the dangers of individualism: loneliness for those who are called the possessors, a feeling of individual guilt for those who do not come off as well.

CLASSLESS SOCIETIES

In his later years, Leo Tolstoy came to believe in a universal human dignity; he also perceived a peculiar way society could tarnish this dignity. There is a telling incident in *Anna Karenina* in which Levin, racked by doubts about his own reasons for living, goes into the fields to cut wheat with the peasants; the work makes Levin forget himself, and great calm and inner acceptance come over him. Levin does not, however, feel *like* a peasant at this moment; his peasants, in fact, seem even more strange to him than before, for now, cutting the wheat and finding himself all absorbed, Levin feels he cannot deduce anything about who these other workers are.

What the Enlightenment thinkers failed to create was an image of human dignity without a face. Once the character of a dignified man becomes in any way tangible, every man is saddled with the obligation to compare his own features to that ideal. To define what is dignified about mankind, rather than take it as an act of faith, sets up the machinery of individualism, for every man enters into the comparative process in order to be rewarded by feeling, and being treated as, a person with dignity. The parable of Levin in the fields was for Tolstoy a picture of how human dignity becomes faceless: this occurs not when men merge into one another, not when they feel that "through work we become as one"; it is rather when their work, their productive actions, are so structured that there is no justification through works. Work loses a larger meaning.

Why is destroying concrete images of dignified living then a matter of destroying classes? Tocqueville, after all, posed the prospect of an America without classes—an "equality of conditions"—yet one where people still remained restless unto death, forever seeking to find some manner of living in which they felt authentic, worthy of being respected, dignified. Equality of conditions, he wrote, does not dampen the evils of individualism; to the contrary, he thought in America equality would lead to an increase in individual anxiety and self-doubt. A modern social commentator, Robert Nisbet, has said that in this, Tocqueville created a picture of status insecurity outside the boundaries of class analysis.

America has not, however, become a society where an equality of conditions prevails, and Tocqueville's psychology of personal worth has come to have its uses in maintaining inequality and economic productivity along class lines. In addition to the old material incentives, the striving to become a developed, and therefore respect-able, person is an incentive that keeps men consuming and working hard. The goal now for most individuals is not to possess, to own, to wield power; instead, material things are aids to creating an inner self which is complex, variegated, not easily fathomed by others—because only with such psychological armor can a person hope to establish some freedom within the terms of a class society. Individualism of this class-bound, defensive kind is what Tolstoy's parable is aimed against.

As we have argued throughout this book, the power of class today is not that it makes individual psychology reflect the behavior of the "system"—we reject, for instance, Marcuse's idea that people on the bottom have tastes similar to those on the top, and therefore keep the Establishment alive. Rather, the way in which people try to keep free of the emotional grip of the social structure, unintentionally, systematically, in aggregate keeps the class order going.

Indeed, some social thinkers now believe it is foolish to talk of an end to social position through symbols of self-development, foolish to hope for Tolstoy's world, because in modern "post-industrial" society inner intellectual development becomes the direct basis for economic growth. Analysts like Alain Touraine and Daniel Bell claim that economic productivity now will expand only through the prestige system based on personal skills, with the professional intellectual occupying the highest status. In the process of each individual struggling for distinction against an ideal standard of performance in a specialized area, the standard of excellence itself will change, Touraine says; competing individuals will thus create new forms of activity to display their talents, and these new activities will yield new goods and services. We are brutally simplifying Touraine's idea here, but even in a crude form, the prediction of a "post-industrial" society ought to give one pause. The environment of rewards for distinctive ability, as we have seen, is so framed that, when what a person does is recognized by a judge as praiseworthy, the performer doesn't feel that this says something about *him;* his talent exists only as an exhibition, not as a commitment to a task. If a post-industrial system is coming into being, if intellectual competition becomes a necessity for economic growth, there will very likely be an increase in men's feelings of meaninglessness in their actions—the actions which, they are persuaded, they must perform if they are "someday" to feel like their own masters. That is to say, to the extent that this linking of personal dignity and personal ability becomes *more* productive economically, estrangements from meaningful action are going to mark the tone of the culture ever more strongly.

The more we have pondered this prediction, the more we have asked ourselves questions whose answers are beyond the scope of this book. If you wish to stop the injuries of class, if you wish to break the links between dignity, freedom, and ability, how do you do away with situations in which people are rewarded by others for what they can do? That, and only that, would be true classlessness; but what, specifically, would have to be done?

The historical record is not reassuring. The Soviet system, for example, can arrive at a state of affairs embodied in the street-sweeper's remark because it still gives rewards for competence; in contrast to an overtly class society like the United States, rewards are either transferred from the individual to competing units of labor or given in the larger society to especially productive and "meritorious" individuals.

In the last decade, among the newer socialist countries, many attempts have been made to divorce personal competence from common dignity. Collective farms with communal work and living arrangements have attempted to link a sense of fraternity with a variety of human skills. People rotate in and out of many administrative and technical jobs in some countries; technicians, bureaucrats, and other white-collar workers are required to do some manual work annually. Cuba and China, most notably, have encouraged as many people as possible to perform the functions of doctors or teachers themselves, either as individuals or in collectives.

Both these countries, however, are pressed by economic scarcity and therefore require central administration and structures of higher authority to deal as efficiently as possible with scarce resources. These countries are trying to avoid the pitfalls of the Soviet experience, where material incentives and emphasis on merit were reintroduced shortly after the revolution in an attempt to increase production. Yet because of the economic situation in these countries, the temptation remains strong to continue the use of comparative, albeit moral, incentives. Comparative moral incentives, as the Soviet experience shows, still serve to undercut self-esteem, and can be extraordinarily repressive.

The United States, however, is not at all in this position; its productive forces have been developed to the point where it can produce far beyond the line of scarcity even with factories and shops working below full capacity. And just as the United States has developed a productive capacity that transcends the regimen of scarcity, so it has developed a greater potential for destroying the very judgmental process itself. This is because an affluent society can afford what no Third World nation can—to be inefficient.

It has often been argued that judgments of ability, and of personal worth to an organization, have been necessary to build the productive efficiency of the Western nations—that inequality is justified on the grounds of the higher output it has made possible. Affluent societies, however, have crossed a line beyond which that justification, were it ever true at all, no longer matters. The problem confronting an affluent capitalist society is not how to make more things, but how to get rid of what it has. The fact that the United States has arrived at a condition where so much more can be produced than is needed means this country can also afford to stop the divisive process of evaluation without threatening survival. We can now afford, if that is the term, to recognize a diversity, rather than a hierarchy of talents, that is, do away with shaming; it is no longer necessary, if it ever was, for organizations to make a few individuals into the "best" and treat the rest as an undifferentiated mass.

It is sometimes argued that a hierarchy of rewards is necessary because different tasks are more or less desirable. Yet if you have to reward people to get them to do noxious or dangerous jobs, isn't that really to say that human beings shouldn't have to do such work at all, and our vaunted technical expertise should be directed to making the innately obnoxious jobs the work of machines?

Can people be expected to work without hierarchical rewards, without symbols of achievement? Look at the split within themselves made by people when they felt threatened by the acceptance of an organization: What fled to an interior life was their loving, because love was violated when they were working for rewards from someone else. Could it be that, in abolishing a hierarchy of rewards, a society might bring these feelings back into the productive forms of men's lives?

The Enlightenment writers sought a humane society through means that came to aid the inhumanities of class. The prophets of a post-industrial society say those inhumanities will increase in the name of technological development. Surely one does not have to think of flight from the modern world, surely it is within the realm of economic and social possibility, to overturn a society based on validations of self, on rewards for performance, on the linking of dignity to special ability. Efface standards of dignity, in order to create an actual feeling of dignity threading man to man—Tolstoy's dictum seems utopian, but the plea of the people who appear in this book is that the utopia is emotionally necessary, right now.

AFTERWORD

by Jonathan Cobb

In this afterword, I would like to explore certain conditions of people's lives that structure the feelings of adequacy and the personal responsibility a person takes for his social position. These are conditions that both surround the moral meanings people bestow on their actions and social position and form much of the content of these interpretations.

Such moral meanings seem to me to exist in another dimension, another system of values that touches on, yet is different from, the issue of whether a person can take care of himself or how he is treated. This dimension is one of social actions, of self-expression organized as social production.

People do not live only in their own personal worlds. John Bertin, the self-sacrificing equipment painter, feels threatened by people on welfare because they threaten him as a necessary being to his wife and children; he fears becoming superfluous in his own home, and therefore being discarded. The janitor Ricca Kartides feels that he is "nothing" compared to the office people after whom he cleans up, that he does nothing important compared to them. Although these feelings bear on the issue of any particular individual's abilities, self-image, and identity, this is not, I believe, the ultimate source of these comparisons. For the worthiness granted a person, and that he sometimes accepts as his own, is not an abstraction all-internal to the self, nor a purely relative issue of different personal abilities, but stems from the social value placed on his labors.

It is the person deemed most productive qualitatively, and within any context, quantitatively, that has come to be seen as the most worthy; this is the social standard established by the bourgeois revolutions, replacing the aristocratic ideal of the cultured individual who develops a refined way of life, who treats himself as an object of art. But no revolution is total; sometimes something new is added, but most often the old is melted down and recast in new molds. The individual as a work of art became the man who makes himself self-sufficient through his actions, and appears finally as the man who "makes something" of himself—that is, a thing for exhibition.

The degree of worthiness granted a person has come to be, in other words, a measurement of his productivity, a personal reflection of the social uses he makes of his time. The human, that is to say social, sense of this worthiness is experienced in relative terms, in terms of who is worth more or less than you are. But the source of this standard is not to be found in identities, but takes its meaning from, and indeed is determined by, calculations of a person's social productivity. The comparisons of worthiness people make with one another spring from this; the hidden question behind "Am I as good as he is?" becomes "Am I as socially valuable as he is? Is my time worth as much as his?"

Deference in American society has this at its root: a calculation that someone else's time is more valuable than your own, which seems to give that person the right to command your time in accordance with his needs. The most obvious example occurs in offices, where it seems right for secretaries to perform services for their superior, not because they respect him as self-sufficient or because they are awed by his abilities, but because the superior's work is considered more valuable than her typing, and so his time more valuable than hers. This is also what makes it seem so "right" for a teacher to give more attention to those who appear more intelligent, because they seem to her potentially so much more valuable and worth her time; and this is the specific sense of moral hierarchy she conveys to her students. For the workingmen with whom we spoke, deference within the family and neighborhood has become overshadowed by these calculations of productivity.

Beyond all consideration of personal feelings of inadequacy, therefore, the hierarchy of social legitimacy in American society has its origin in these calculations of social value. It is not ability as such that legitimizes a child as a person with special rights in the family, but the child's possession of those talents considered more productive by the world outside the family. Feeling that you are a legitimate actor in the world, that is, a person with social rights, comes from feeling that what you do, whether in concert with or opposition to others, has value. It is not, then, the act of self-sacrifice as such that legitimizes a person like John Bertin as a man with social rights, but the fact that his work is socially productive. Work organized as self-sacrifice, however, causes this sense of legitimacy to assume a particular form— self-righteousness.

It is a myth that people do things only for themselves, as

the whole notion of sacrifice goes to show. But a person like Bertin is working for more than his family, too, no matter what the conscious direction towards which he organizes his labors. He works for others outside his family by the very nature of his job—for his employer, of course, but that only serves to conceal the valuable services he performs for others. And the social definitions he makes about his work center around a need to feel that he is socially useful, a need to feel that he contributes something to others in the society in which he lives. That need to feel socially useful is, in its turn, rooted in the fact that people are interdependent on one another for fulfillment of their personal, social, and economic needs.

Social usefulness, as both socially determined—that is, what other people think is important—and as a personally determined value, is another dimension of the interpretations people make of their lives. The garbage man who says he is "just a poor slob" means in the first place that he has not developed the powers that he feels higher-class people have, that he feels inadequate as a person in comparison; but he also means that he is superfluous in terms of what "really" happens in society, of "real" social contributions, that he as an active man, not just a moral one, does not count and is, therefore, "nothing." To ignore this is to miss all the feelings of marginality among many of the workers with whom we spoke, from those who wished they were part of the "capitalist class" to those who feared being left behind by upper-class people: "If they get ahead so much, with their money and with everything else, they're going to leave a lot of people behind." Almost all the invidious comparisons people make of each other in American society pass through the medium of production. That one person compares himself to another, using his powers to control or shame another person, as in conveying the sense that "I am more developed than you are," is the outcome of what development is considered to be in the field of social production. Conversely, the sense of social failure that we found among the people with whom we talked had, to my mind, these same two dimensions: on the one hand, it was an expression of a closure in a person's life, a feeling that he as a person was not growing; on the other, it was a sense that he had failed to contribute anything of real value to the society in which he lives. The two go hand in hand because people live in the world, and are social creatures. Every question of identity as an image of social place in a hierarchy is also a question of social value. The medium that unites them is a person's activity, which says something about the person and is a projection into the world.

The meanings a person makes and receives about what he or she does, center around this same issue of the social production of value. For the teacher, it is believing that teaching is a socially valuable activity (is that not what "doing good" means for the teacher—helping people to grow, but with an eye towards the larger society?), for the artist it is believing that art has value; while for the factory worker, for the janitor, for the clerical worker, it is believing that productive work is valuable. That is, for workingpeople, it is work in general, as opposed to any specific skill, that is seen to give a person a sense of legitimacy, whereas for persons of higher class, it is a specific function that is seen as legitimizing. In either case, however, the source of social legitimacy in capitalist society comes primarily from what a person produces, and it is from this that inferences are drawn about who he essentially *is*.

The organization of lives in terms of social production for private profit forms the ground on which the factory, the office, and the school system are organized. In the school, the development of powers in the person, aside from any intrinsic goodness, is oriented towards making people as productive as possible within the terms of the existing society. It is in school that different skills are first experienced as arranged in a hierarchy of value—that doing well in physics is seen to count so much more than playing the guitar well. The goal towards which all education is oriented is social productivity, but this is put in terms of a personal development of abilities. What comes finally to be most important to the teacher is not the abstract potential she or he sees in students, but how much of that potential is being concretely realized as shown by actual classroom performance, by what approved powers the students do in fact demonstrate.

Today a man is known by his ability, not as abstract essence, but as concrete demonstration. The educational degree certifies that you are capable of demonstrating "ability," meaning that you can concretely apply yourself to particular tasks that are considered to demand more skill, and deemed more valuable, than the ordinary. The qualitative differences in abilities, in different kinds of work, have become an issue because of the increasing social division of labor, where different tasks call for different skills. When everyone does roughly the same kind of task, in a society based on competition, it is quantity of production that becomes the issue; when tasks are differentiated, it is qualitative production that matters. It is professional, management, and technical skills that have today come to be seen as more socially valuable than manual or clerical labor—socially valuable in two senses: first, that they seem so distinctive and stand out as individualized contributions that are noticed and effective in society as a whole; second, in the sense that more social time was spent on cultivating the development of a skilled person, an educated person, than on that of a manual worker.

This respect for distinctive ability tends to take on a life of its own—that is to say, the means for the production of social value become taken for ends in themselves. And indeed, it is precisely the continual demonstrations of worthiness that serve to make ability appear as an end in itself. When we consider ability not in itself but as a social value, however, the issue becomes transformed from one of ability to one of moral values and politics. It is this artificial separation of questions of ability from questions of value in our analyses that makes so many social processes so mystifying. In our everyday attitudes, this artificial separation does not exist, because the values are tacit. Someone is considered "better" both in the sense of competence and in that of having, or acting in accordance with, higher values: the teachers of working-class kids with whom we spoke talked about their students as having both less ability and "lower" values than others. The uses of ability, of development, of culture, are political questions, questions about which the ruling class in any age sets the standards. Because of their monopoly in this regard, because their particular values appear as universal, it becomes a matter of having "culture" or not having it, of having "ability" or not having it, rather than of having different cultures, different values, different developments, different abilities. To be caught in a schema of particular values, to live under the terms set only by others, is to feel inadequate in relation to those others. This is the ground upon which feelings of inadequacy, as opposed to feelings merely of difference, arise.

But it is the uses to which ability and development are put that structures how people live from day to day, and their personal identities. The workingpeople with whom we talked spoke bitterly about their sense of people not caring for each other, but being interested instead only in their own development. The kids in the Watson School didn't feel betrayed only because others were getting approval, but because they felt the Freds and Vincents were using their powers and that approval not towards aiding them, but towards escaping the situation and progressing by themselves. The image of individualism as the only means for survival and self-development is formed out of experiences of desertion by others who have needs similar to your own. It is in this way that identity comes to be conceived of as a matter of accumulation for your own development, and further, development in contradistinction to others. It is the attitudes formed under these conditions that provide the basis for criticizing others as selfish and materialistic, while at the same time you feel the necessity to act likewise in order to protect yourself. Ricca Kartides, for example, believes that others have shown a lack of consideration for him because of their intentions, while he fails to show consideration for others only when he is driven to it. It is in this way that each is led to impugn the motives of the other, because each can only get somewhere by leaving others behind.

To talk of arming yourself, of the development of self-confidence, of self-development on the terms set by the existing society, is to talk about what seems possible in the society as what seems *ipso facto* legitimate. When the structure of society appears as permanent or beyond human control, when what human beings have created comes to seem immutable, "natural," transformation becomes individualized. How *you* are going to interpret the world moves to the front of consciousness, how you can transform it in accordance with your needs ceases to be a real question. This is the context in which all questions of personal and social legitimacy occur. American society is characterized by an appearance of permanence as a system, but by a reality of permeability by individuals.

This permeability, however, has its own inherent limitations: the person does not come to exercise control over his situation, transforming the conditions of his or her life, but instead simply moves from one set of circumstances to another. Circumstances, the structure of society, remains and you move; and as a result, you leave situations, classes, structures, as they are. Thus, someone like James the college student, who does not seem to feel particularly inadequate or insecure, plans to deal with the contradiction between his expectations of college life and its reality by moving from one major to another, staying in school, creating a slightly different life style in order to survive with some sense of personal growth. Because he can see himself moving in society he individually looks for another situation, rather than transforming the one he is in.

RELATED WRITINGS
OF INTEREST

Argyris, Chris. *Personality and Organization: The Conflict Between System and the Individual.* New York: Harper Torchbooks, Harper & Row, 1970.

Bakke, E. Wight. *The Unemployed Worker.* Yale University Press, 1940.

Management in the Course of Industrialization. New York: Harper Torchbooks, Harper & Row, 1963.

Berg, Ivar. *Education and Jobs: The Great Training Robbery.* New York: Praeger, 1970.

Berger, Bennett M. *Working-Class Suburb: A Study of Auto Workers in Suburbia.* Berkeley and Los Angeles: University of California Press, 1968.

Blau, Peter M., and Otis Dudley Duncan. *The American Occupational Structure.* New York: John Wiley & Sons, 1967.

Blauner, Robert. *Alienation and Freedom: The Factory Worker and His Industry.* Chicago and London: Phoenix Books, University of Chicago Press, 1967.

Bonnell, Victoria, and Michael Reich. *Workers in the American Economy: Data on the Labor Force.* Boston: New England Free Press, 1969.

Bottomore, T. B. *Classes in Modern Society.* New York: Vintage Books, Random House, 1966.

Bottomore, T. B., ed. *Karl Marx: Early Writings.* New York: McGraw-Hill Book Company, 1964.

Bronfenbrenner, Urie. *Two Worlds of Childhood: U.S. and U.S.S.R.* New York: Russell Sage Foundation, 1970.

Related Writings of Interest

Cawelti, John G. *Apostles of the Self-Made Man: Changing Concepts of Success in America*. Chicago and London: University of Chicago Press, 1968.

Centers, Richard. *The Psychology of Social Classes: A Study of Class Consciousness*. New York: Russell & Russell, 1961.

Chinoy, Ely. *Automobile Workers and the American Dream*. Boston: Beacon Press, 1968.

Friedmann, Georges. *Industrial Society: The Emergence of the Human Problems of Automation*. New York: Free Press of Glencoe, 1955.

Gans, Herbert J. *The Urban Villagers: Group and Class in the Life of Italian-Americans*. New York: Free Press of Glencoe, 1962.

Ginzberg, Eli, and Hyman Berman. *The American Worker in the Twentieth Century: A History Through Autobiographies*. New York: Free Press of Glencoe, 1963.

Glazer, Nathan, and Daniel Patrick Moynihan. *Beyond the Melting Pot: The Negroes, Puerto Ricans, Jews, Italians, and Irish of New York City*. Cambridge, Massachusetts: M.I.T. Press, 1964.

Goldthorpe, John H., David Lockwood, Frank Bechhofer, and Jennifer Platt. *The Affluent Worker in the Class Structure*. Cambridge, England: Cambridge University Press, 1969.

Gordon, Milton M. *Assimilation in American Life: The Role of Race, Religion and National Origins*. New York: Oxford University Press, 1964.

Grier, William H., and Price M. Cobbs. *Black Rage*. New York: Bantam Books, published by arrangement with Basic Books, 1969.

Hamilton, Richard F. *Affluence and the French Worker in the Fourth Republic*. Princeton: Princeton University Press, 1967.

Handlin, Oscar. *Boston's Immigrants, 1790–1880: A Study in Acculturation.* New York: Atheneum, 1969.

Hollingshead, A. B. *Elmtown's Youth: Impact of Social Classes on Adolescents.* New York: John Wiley & Sons, 1967.

Inkeles, Alex, and Raymond Bauer. *The Soviet Citizen: Daily Life in a Totalitarian Society.* New York: Atheneum, 1968.

Jacobs, Paul. *The State of the Unions.* New York: Atheneum, 1966.

Jencks, Christopher, and David Riesman. *The Academic Revolution.* Garden City, New York: Doubleday & Company, 1969.

Kohn, Melvin L. *Class and Conformity: A Study in Values.* Homewood, Illinois: Dorsey Press, 1969.

Komorovsky, Mirra. *Blue-Collar Marriage.* New York: Vintage Books, Random House, 1967.

Lefebvre, Henri. *Everyday Life in the Modern World.* New York: Harper Torchbooks, Harper & Row, 1971.

Leggett, John C. *Class, Race, and Labor: Working Class Consciousness in Detroit.* New York: Oxford University Press, 1968.

Lynd, Helen Merrell. *On Shame and the Search for Identity.* New York: John Wiley & Sons, 1967.

Lynd, Robert S., and Helen Merrell Lynd. *Middletown: A Study in Modern American Culture.* New York: Harcourt, Brace & World, 1929.

Lynd, Robert S., and Helen Merrell Lynd. *Middletown in Transition: A Study in Cultural Conflicts.* New York: Harcourt, Brace & World, 1937.

Mishler, Elliot G., and Nancy E. Waxler. *Interaction in Families: An Experimental Study of Family Processes and Schizophrenia.* New York: John Wiley & Sons, 1968.

Related Writings of Interest

Ossowski, Stanislaw. *Class Structure in the Social Consciousness.* New York: Free Press of Glencoe, 1963.

Sayles, Leonard R. *Managerial Behavior: Administration in Complex Organizations.* New York: McGraw-Hill Book Company, 1964.

Sexton, Patricia Cayo. *The Feminized Male: Classrooms, White Collars and the Decline of Manliness.* New York: Vintage Books, Random House, 1970.

Terkel, Studs. *Hard Times: An Oral History of the Great Depression.* New York: Avon Books, by arrangement with Pantheon Books, Random House, 1971.

Thernstrom, Stephan. *Poverty and Progress: Social Mobility in a Nineteenth Century City.* New York: Atheneum, 1969.

Thompson, E. P. *The Making of the English Working Class.* New York: Vintage Books, Random House, 1963.

Weber, Max. *The Protestant Ethic and the Spirit of Capitalism.* New York: Charles Scribner's Sons, 1958.

Weiss, Richard. *The American Myth of Success: From Horatio Alger to Norman Vincent Peale.* New York: Basic Books, 1969.

Willmott, Peter. *Adolescent Boys of East London.* Baltimore, Maryland: Pelican Books, Penguin Books, 1966.

Young, Michael. *The Rise of the Meritocracy.* Baltimore, Maryland: Pelican Books, Penguin Books, 1965.

Zeitlin, Maurice. *Revolutionary Politics and the Cuban Working Class.* Princeton: Princeton University Press, 1967.

Zweig, Ferdynand. *The Worker in an Affluent Society: Family Life and Industry.* New York: Free Press of Glencoe, 1962.

A NOTE ABOUT THE AUTHORS

Richard Sennett was born in Chicago in 1943, and took his bachelor's degree at the University of Chicago (1964) and his Ph.D. at Harvard (1969). He teaches sociology at New York University. He is the author of *The Uses of Disorder* and *Families Against the City*, co-author of *Nineteenth Century Cities*, and editor of *Classic Essays on the Culture of Cities*, in addition to being a frequent contributor to *The New York Times Book Review* and the *New York Review of Books*. Mr. Sennett began his career as a musician, and is presently working on a book about artists and cities. He lives in New York City.

Jonathan Cobb was born in 1946 in Summit, New Jersey. He received his B.A. from Columbia University in 1969. Since then he has been involved in working-class studies at the Center for the Study of Public Policy in Cambridge, Massachusetts. Mr. Cobb and his wife live with six other people in Dorchester, Massachusetts.